PARANORMAL BLACK COUNTRY

RICHARD O'CONNOR

AMBERLEY

First published 2025

Amberley Publishing
The Hill, Stroud
Gloucestershire, GL5 4EP

www.amberley-books.com

British Library Cataloguing in Publication Data.
A catalogue record for this book is available from the British Library.

ISBN 978 1 3981 1941 3 (print)
ISBN 978 1 3981 1942 0 (ebook)

Typesetting by Hurix Digital, India.
Printed in Great Britain.

Appointed GPSR EU Representative: Easy Access System Europe Oü, 16879218
Address: Mustamäe tee 50, 10621, Tallinn, Estonia
Contact Details: gpsr.requests@easproject.com, +358 40 500 3575

Contents

Introduction

The story of the Black Country begins hundreds of millions of years ago, when much of England, then positioned near the equator, was a tropical shallow sea where trilobites, ammonites and other long-extinct creatures thrived. When they died, their remains accumulated on the seabed alongside countless other organisms. Over the aeons that followed, their remains were transformed into the coal that powered the Industrial Revolution in the eighteenth century. The South Staffordshire coalfield emerged as one of the country's largest and most accessible coalfields, supplying the fuel for the ironworking foundries and forges that veiled the region in black smoke. From this industrious landscape, the Black Country was forged. Yet, the Black Country is more than just a cradle of fire and ore. People have called the region home for thousands of years, during which it has become rich with stories of ghosts and supernatural legends.

Defining the Black Country's boundaries is a topic of debate. Some argue it should be confined to the coalfield area. For this book, however, we will venture a little further, exploring the four metropolitan boroughs of Dudley, Sandwell, West Bromwich, and Wolverhampton, which form the modern definition of the Black

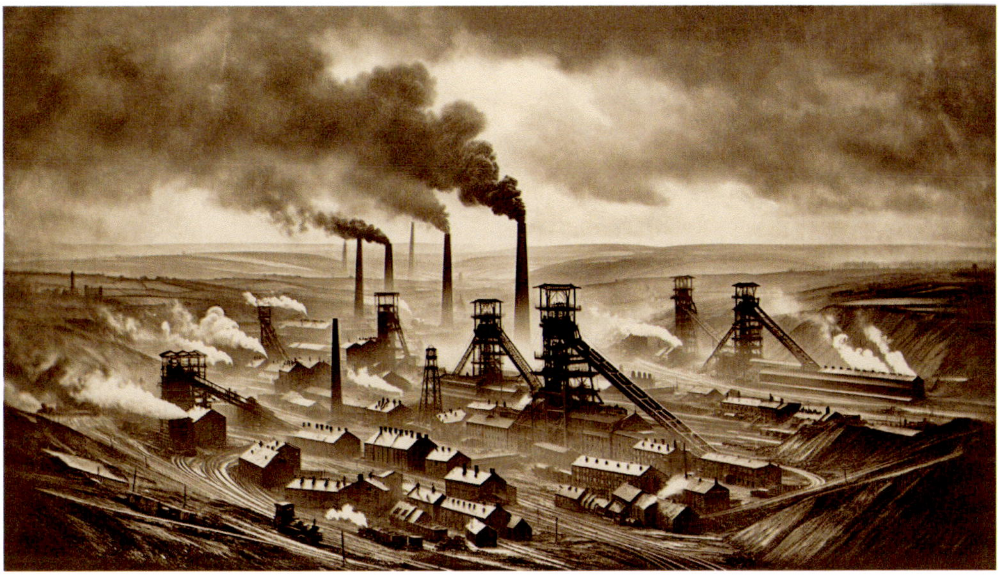

The skyline over the Black Country was once dominated by collieries that filled the skies with the black smoke from which the region gets its name.

Country. In any case, it's a big place, and capturing its paranormal heritage in full isn't possible in a single book like this. The stories that follow are a mixture of some of the region's most famous tales and legends, along with some new stories from those I've met and spoken with along the journey.

As someone who was born in the Black Country, I feel honoured to have the opportunity to write about its ghostly tales and revisit some of the places where I spent the first half of my childhood. So, before we embark on this tour, I'd like to express my deepest gratitude to all those who have made this book possible. This includes the individuals who generously shared their stories or photographs, the newspaper archives that were invaluable sources of historical tales, and my friend Ian Holt, whose assistance in finding the right words was indispensable. I must also extend a special thank you to my wife, Sandy, for her unwavering patience and enthusiasm. And lastly, I am grateful to you, the reader, for choosing this book, a labour of love I devoted many hours to over the course of a year. I hope you find the stories within as captivating as I have.

Dudley

Our journey through the haunted Black Country begins in the borough of Dudley, with the town of Dudley regarded, by some, as the capital of the Black Country. As one of the birthplaces of the Industrial Revolution, the transformative era shifted Dudley from a historic market town to a hub of industry. While the coal, iron, and limestone industries are now resigned to its history, the town remains home to thousands of people, many of whom have eerie tales to tell.

In 1997, residents of the Prince of Wales tower block in St James's Terrace reported a haunting that disrupted their lives. The typical signs were there: a sofa moving by itself, lights flickering on and off, and even a gas cooker turning on of its own accord. The presence also manifested as dark shadows darting across walls. Initially reported by a resident on the eleventh floor of the twenty-storey building, the ghost was quickly exorcised but then seemed to move to a flat on the fourth floor. The Prince of Wales tower block was demolished two years later, finally taking the persistent spirit with it.

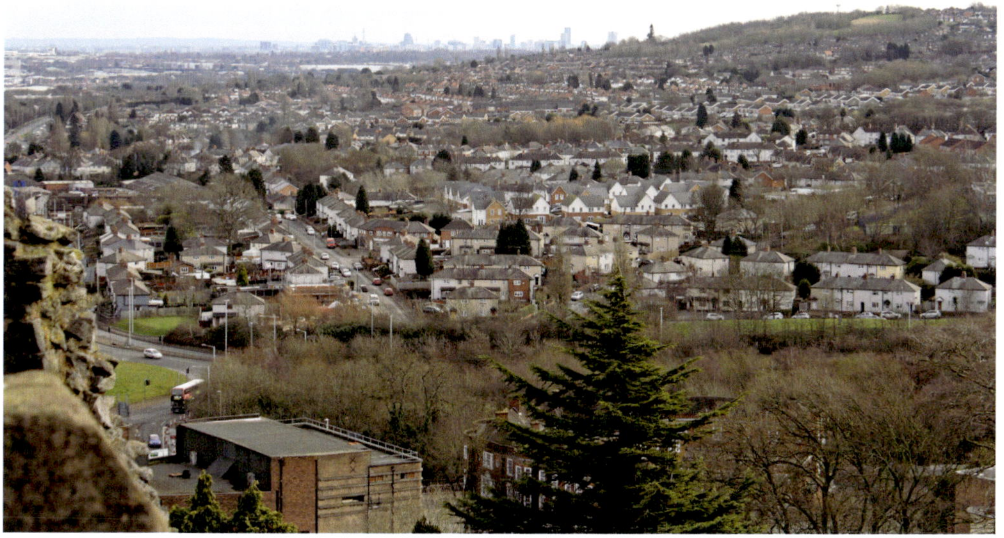

The view of Dudley from Dudley Castle, looking towards Birmingham.

A little over a mile away, in Upper Gornal, a phantom physician was troubling workmen restoring an eighteenth-century house in 1985. During the renovations, tools were reportedly moving around the room on their own, and timbers were hurled at the workers by an unseen entity. Some witnessed a shadowy figure in a doorway and heard heavy footsteps on the floorboards. Eventually, the workmen grew accustomed to the spirit, considering it just another occupational hazard. The site owner speculated that it could be the ghost of a doctor, linking back to the building's history as a surgery and chemist's shop.

However, Dudley also boasts some of the oldest and most impressive buildings in the Black Country region, alongside its share of famous hauntings.

Dudley Castle and Zoo

In 1645 at the height of the English Civil War, the Parliamentary army laid siege to Dudley Castle. In September, Dorothy, wife of second-in-command Lieutenant-Colonel John Beaumont, was recorded as having a child 'borne and bury'd' on the same day and laid to rest at St Edmund's Church just outside the castle walls. As the siege continued and days turned into weeks, Dorothy grew increasingly fragile of mind. On occasion, she wandered the castle grounds, hopelessly searching for baby Frances, convinced she had been mislaid or kidnapped.

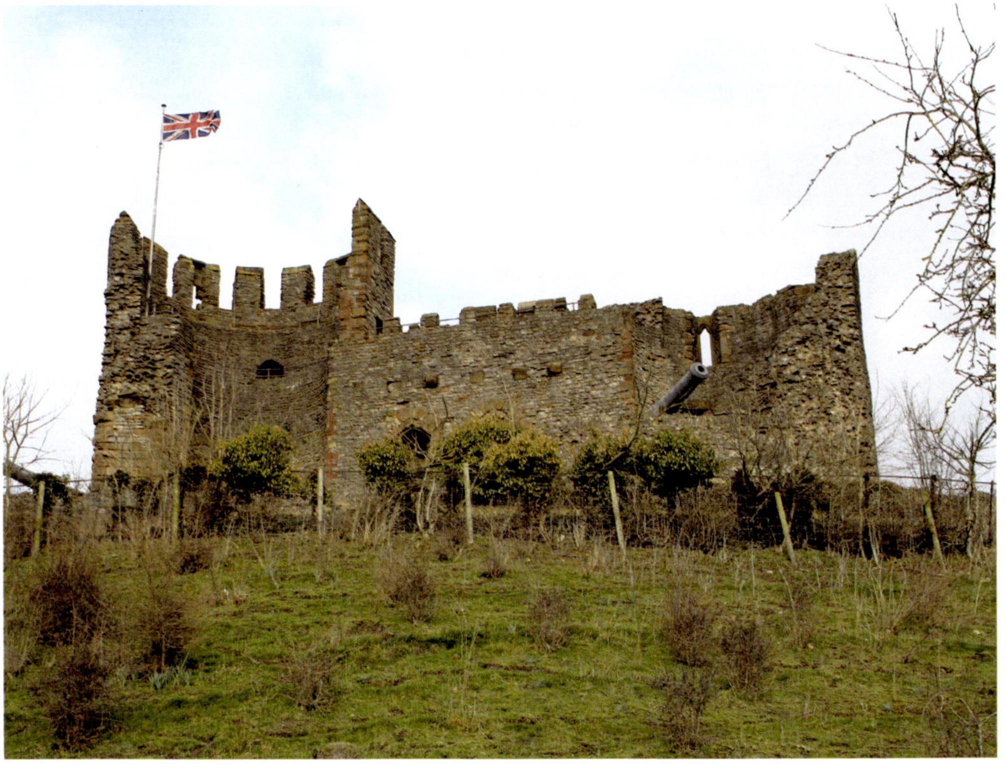

Dudley Castle.

On 26 April, seven months after the death of Frances, Dorothy too passed away, and having come to terms with her daughter's death, made two dying wishes. First, she asked to be buried next to her daughter, and second, for her husband to be present at her funeral. Neither happened. The invading Roundheads destroyed St Edmund's to create a wider field of aim for their cannons and refused to allow her husband, the second commanding officer of their enemy, to leave the castle unharmed in the middle of their brutal war. Ever since, Dorothy's restless spirit is said to roam the castle grounds.

In October 1966, a nineteen-year-old man employed at the castle's restaurant called the police in a state of shock, reporting 'weird noises' and a shape approaching him from the castle keep. The shape was described as a grey figure. The Grey Lady of Dudley Castle, as she became known, has been seen many times since and is believed by many to be Dorothy Beaumont.

Although rarely captured on camera, the best photographic evidence of the Grey Lady was from 2014, when a grey figure appeared in a doorway of the Tudor part of the castle. The area is cordoned off to all because of falling masonry, ruling out the possibility of it being another visitor or castle tour guide in costume. The Grey Lady is closely linked with another of the castle's famous ghosts, the Drummer Boy.

On a sunny February morning in 2023, I met Amy Hickman, a historian and guide who works at the castle and arguably knows more about its ghosts than anyone. As we walked through the historic castle grounds, Amy described the events that, over 300 years ago, led to the Drummer Boy's unfortunate demise. Witnesses describe him as a young man in an old Civil War uniform, often seen on the steps leading up to a castle gatehouse, where the eternal beat of his drum can still be heard.

When Dorothy Beaumont died, a message needed to be passed to the Parliamentarians requesting safe passage of her coffin to a nearby church for burial. This was the job of the drummer boy, who – Amy said – would have been a trusted sergeant rather than a young boy. He stepped beyond the castle gates, banging his drum, which requested a ceasefire and safe passage to deliver his message. However, a drummer boy sent by the Parliamentarians in response was shot and killed. The furious Roundheads told the Royalists they could bury Dorothy's coffin, but only allowed them twenty minutes to complete their task. A walk to the church from the castle takes around ten to fifteen minutes, making the task near impossible and leaving the Royalists with no option but to run with the coffin. Remarkably, they made it there and back in the allotted time without a single shot being fired. This event is remembered with a coffin race that occasionally takes place through Dudley town.

Whilst the Grey Lady, seen numerous times, is the castle's most famous ghost, Amy told me that the oldest sighting dates back to 1870, many years before the castle zoo was opened. A small group was taking a private tour of the grounds when a man in seventeenth-century clothes and a top hat was spotted on the ramped path leading up to the castle keep. The castle grounds were not open to the general public at that time, arousing the curiosity and suspicions of the tour guide. The mystery man walked into the castle keep, but when the guide followed with his group to discover the identity of this mysterious intruder, there was no sign of him.

Another encounter in the castle keep was reported in the 1930s. Often called the brown lady, this dark figure is believed to have been a local woman accused of witchcraft. Amy explained that one of the many cruel and superstitious Jacobean

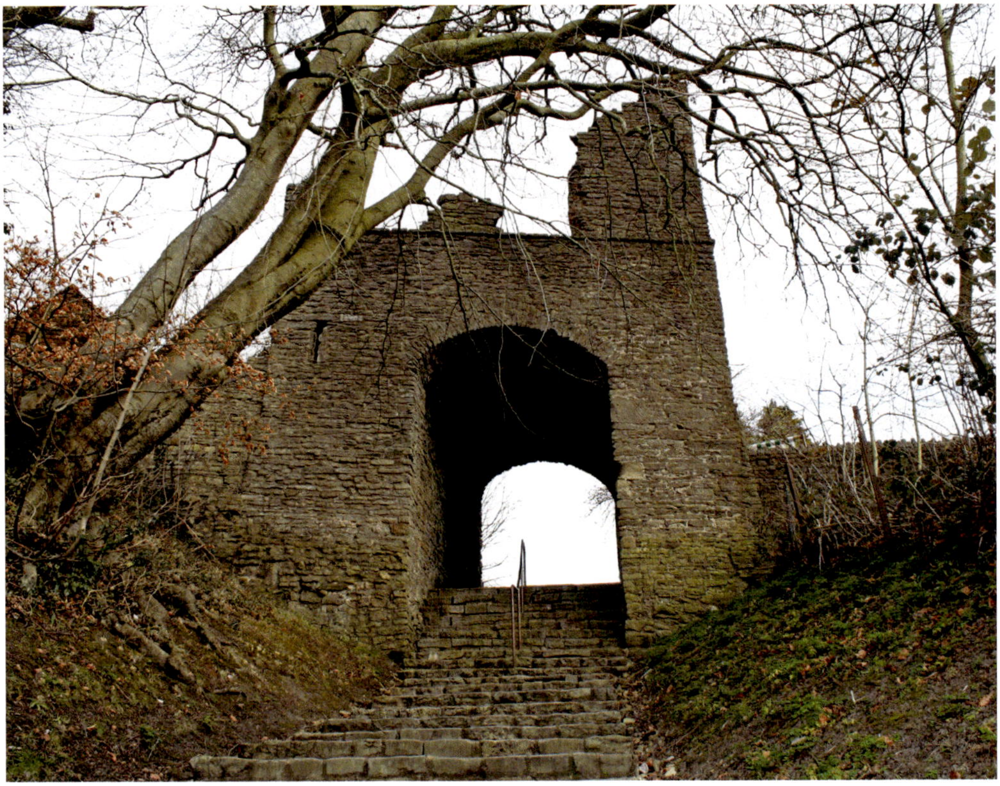

The ghost of the Drummer Boy is most often seen or heard on the steps leading up to the castle.

methods for testing whether a woman was a witch or not was to push her off a tall building. If she were a witch, she'd fly away or at least survive the fall, but if she weren't a witch and died, her innocent soul would go to Heaven anyway. Either way, no harm would come to her self-righteous accusers. It's thought the dark figure seen high up in the castle keep is one such unfortunate woman walking towards her imminent death.

Amy led us to the undercroft, also known as the chapel crypt, considered by many to be the most haunted area within the castle. In August 1953, the *Birmingham Evening Despatch* reported on a series of paranormal investigations centred around the crypt, which was used for the zoo's aquarium at the time. Zookeepers had reported a series of 'queer experiences': doors opening by themselves or refusing to open when pushed, whispers emanating from the walls, and, despite the room being maintained at a consistent 26 degrees Celsius for the tropical fish, unexpected gusts of cold air. Newspapers from as far afield as Canada and the USA reported instances of fish in the aquarium mysteriously switching tanks overnight. Assuming it was the work of pranksters, the police were called in to investigate, but they found 'no marks of forcible entry, no evidence of breaking in, and no fingerprints'.

Despite at least five separate investigations conducted over multiple nights by three independent research groups, the castle's ghosts remained elusive. One team even employed a 'Super Ray' device, which they claimed would emit vibrations when

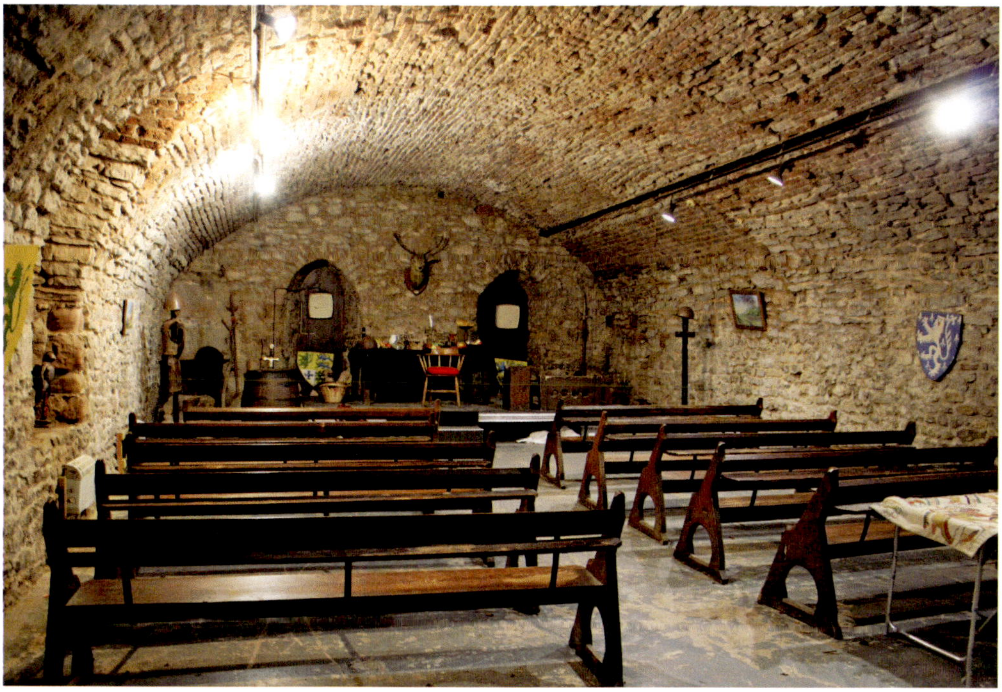

Part of the undercroft at Dudley Castle, home to two stone coffins and possibly the ghost of one of their occupants.

a ghost approached. Yet, the device stayed inactive, even though the paranormal investigators reported hearing unexplainable footsteps in the corner of the crypt, a space once traversed by monks daily.

In another part of the undercroft, two stone coffins – one substantially larger than the other – are positioned in the far corners of the room. The large coffin is believed to belong to John De Somery. The De Somery family owned the castle from 1264 and were permitted by the King to refortify its defences. John, like a modern-day mafia don, raised money for this restoration work through murder and robbery in the local area, and was nicknamed the 'Bad Baron' of Dudley. John, the last of the De Somery line, died without an heir in 1321 and was buried at nearby Dudley Priory.

One morning in 1994, a cleaner on her hands and knees, scrubbing the floor, noticed a pair of old-fashioned spurred boots in her peripheral vision. Initially, she thought it was Mr Durkin, the castle keeper, who often wore period costumes for his guided tours. Without looking up, she greeted him with a friendly 'good morning', but received only a soft chuckle in return. When she finally looked up, she saw the large empty boots standing at the foot of the Bad Baron's coffin. As another cleaner entered the room, the boots disappeared before their eyes. Shocked by the experience, the two cleaners rushed to the on-site restaurant and told the other staff members what they had witnessed. A subsequent search of the area yielded no explanation.

This part of the castle would have been used most often by monks, and visitors have often reported hearing the sounds of their melodic chants. However, the most vivid sighting of monks occurred outside in the courtyard in 1978, when electrical

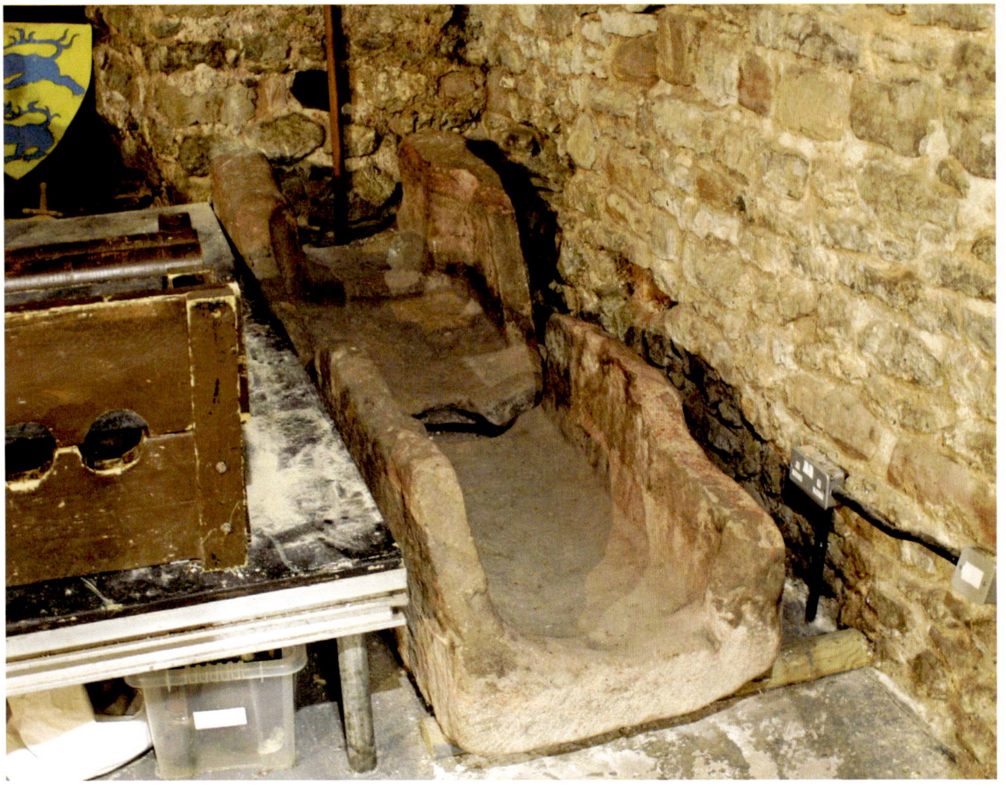

John De Somery's stone coffin.

contractors saw a procession of hooded monks walking towards the chapel building. The workmen fled and refused to come back on site.

The courtyard is also home to Dudley Castle's animal ghost sightings, with one believed to have originated long before the castle became a zoo. Legend states that a small dog accompanied Dorothy Beaumont during her time in the castle. Upon her death, the dog reportedly sat by the castle keep for three days and nights before mysteriously disappearing. The fate of Dorothy's dog remained unknown, but some claimed to have heard the bark of a little dog on the anniversary of her death. Although Amy mentioned never hearing the dog's bark during her anniversary visits, an archaeological excavation in the 1980s discovered the skeleton of a small dog at the base of the castle keep. The remains were carbon-dated to the same period Dorothy lived.

A more alarming sighting is that of a cheetah spotted darting freely around the castle grounds. In the zoo's early days, the castle keeper was Harry Hatch. He lived in the cottage within the castle walls and hand-reared many of the zoo's first animals. Harry's favourite was a cheetah named Shirley, who he used to exercise by running her around the castle courtyard with his dog. This historical fact was unknown to two terrified ladies on a ghost hunt in the early 2000s, who described to Amy their sighting of what looked like a big cat tearing through the courtyard. All enclosures were checked as a matter of safety, but all big cats were accounted for.

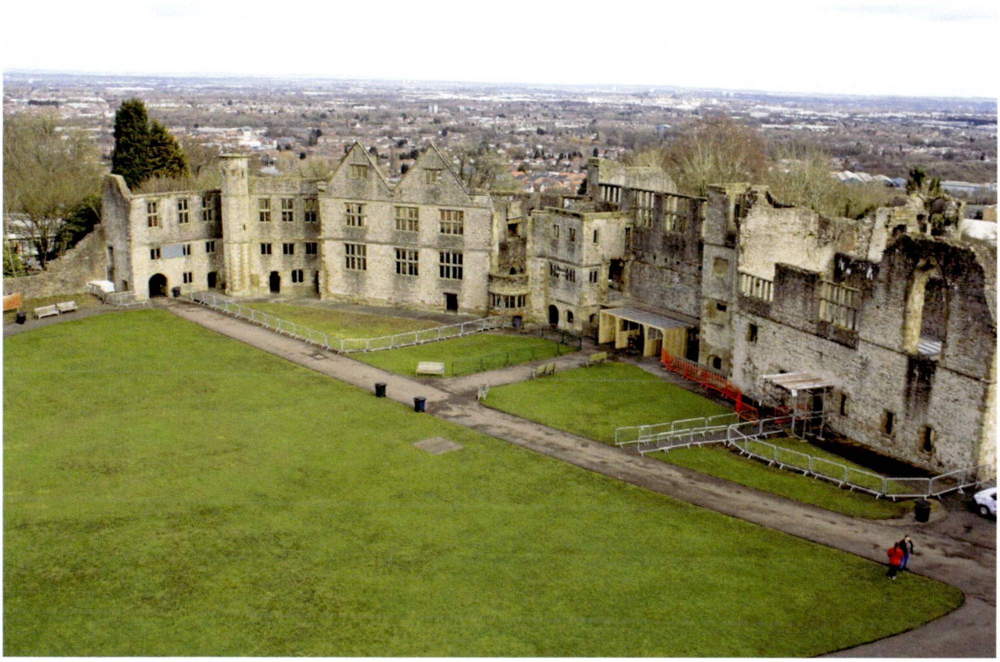

After the Civil War in the 1600s, the castle was partially demolished to prevent it from being used as a defensive stronghold ever again. Some of the residential parts of the building remained, such as the Sharington Range in this photograph, but they, too, were destroyed by fire in 1750.

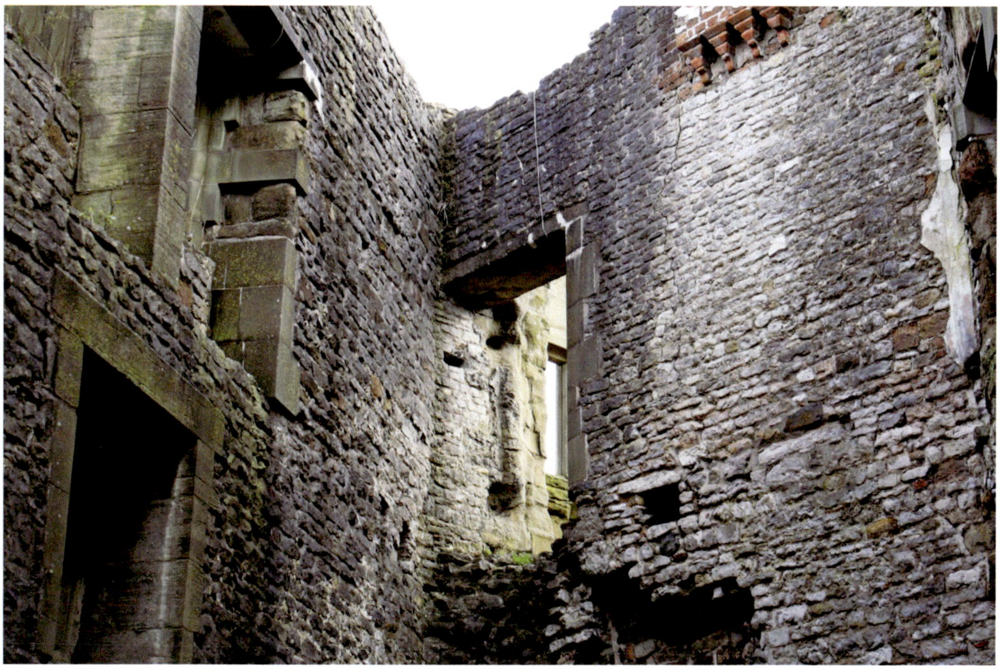

Inside Dudley Castle.

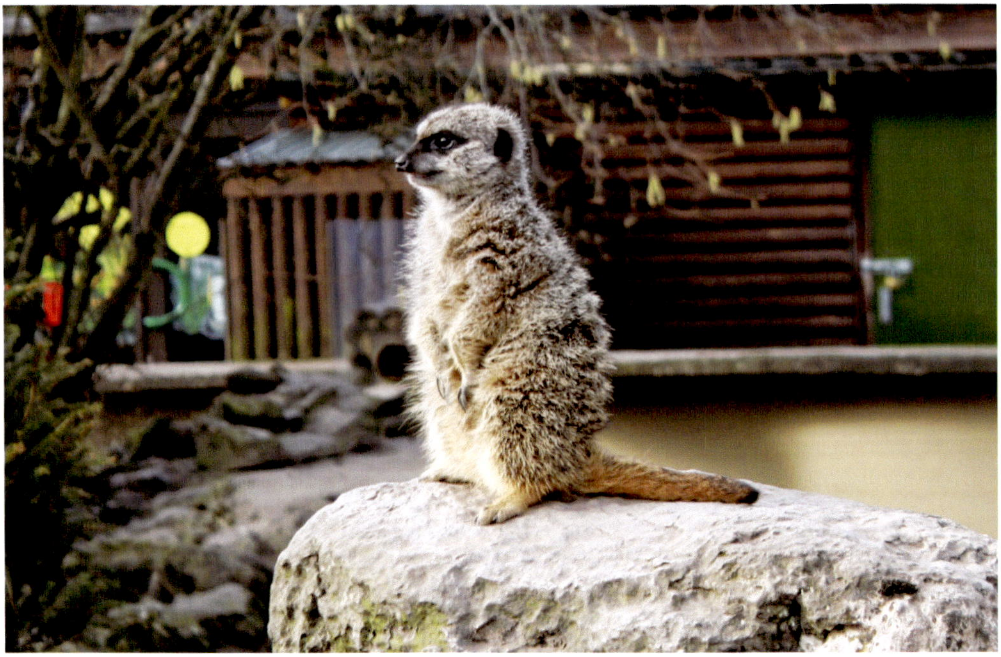

A zoo opened at Dudley Castle in the 1930s, providing a home for thousands of animals.

The Station Hotel

Standing at the foot of Castle Hill in Dudley, The Station Hotel boasts a history deeply resonant with ghostly tales. Indeed, it may claim the title of the most haunted hotel in the Black Country. With such a reputation, I decided the best way to experience its mysterious allure was by booking a room for the night. As I checked in one cold February evening, anticipation and curiosity piqued my interest. Would I encounter a phantom guest from a bygone era or witness the paranormal phenomena that had sent many before me fleeing into the night?

The tale of The Station Hotel dates back to the nineteenth century when Dudley, a thriving industrial town, was rapidly expanding and soon outgrew its then primary hotel, The Castle. Built in 1898, The Station Hotel initially featured a black-and-white facade, complete with a courtyard and stables. Horses drank from a fountain outside the hotel, now relocated to the top of the hill and substituted by traffic lights. The hotel prospered during its golden years, partly thanks to its prime location catering to Dudley's most prestigious attraction, the Opera House. Upper-class patrons from across the West Midlands flocked to be enthralled by the greatest entertainers of the era. Tragically, the Opera House was destroyed by a fire in 1933, only for the Hippodrome to rise from the ashes a few years later, thereby ensuring Dudley would remain a hub of entertainment for generations to come.

The Station Hotel's prime location near the Hippodrome made it the perfect accommodation for some of the biggest stars of the time. Black-and-white photographs of renowned personalities such as Oliver Hardy, Frank Sinatra, Doris Day, George Formby and many more adorn the corridor walls, commemorating their stays at

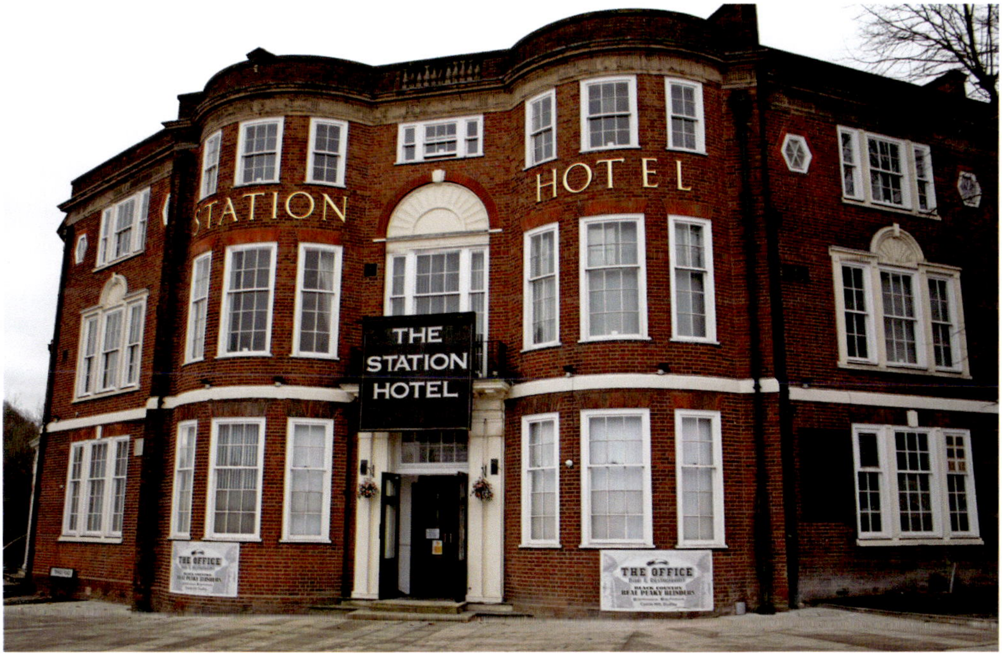

The Station Hotel, Dudley.

the hotel. Famed comedian Tommy Cooper was also a regular guest whenever he performed at the Hippodrome. A long-time friend of his wrote about meeting Tommy in the hotel restaurant, where, before leaving, Tommy asked the waitress, 'Keep me a place for tomorrow.' The next day, Tommy sat at the same table, and the waitress said she'd reserved him a lovely fish. A bewildered Tommy said, 'But I have not ordered fish!' To which she insisted, 'Yes, you did. You asked me to keep you a plaice for today.' Perhaps the Black Country sense of humour was why he loved Dudley so much.

Some of the ghosts reputed to haunt The Station Hotel, however, have a more sinister character. A local landlord is said to have lured a servant girl into the cellar. Legend has it that when she spurned his advances and threatened to inform his wife, the enraged man strangled her and concealed her body in a barrel. I searched extensively for records of the murder or the individuals involved, but found no concrete evidence. In fact, the story appears to be primarily based on spirits allegedly detected by Derek Acorah during a 2003 episode of *Most Haunted*, filmed at the hotel. Nevertheless, many maintain that the cellar is a focal point for paranormal activity, with sightings of both the murderer and his young victim.

In 1995, well before *Most Haunted*'s visit, a ghost walk guide reported seeing the hazy figure of a man dressed in grey and black rush past her and descend the cellar steps. She told reporters from the *Black Country Evening Mail* that, at first, she felt a bit silly mentioning it to hotel staff. When she did, she learned they, too, had seen a similar figure in the same area of the hotel. Two participants on another ghost walk at the hotel saw a similar ghost so vividly they thought it was a part of the show. In more recent years, overnight ghost hunts have concentrated on the cellar area, where

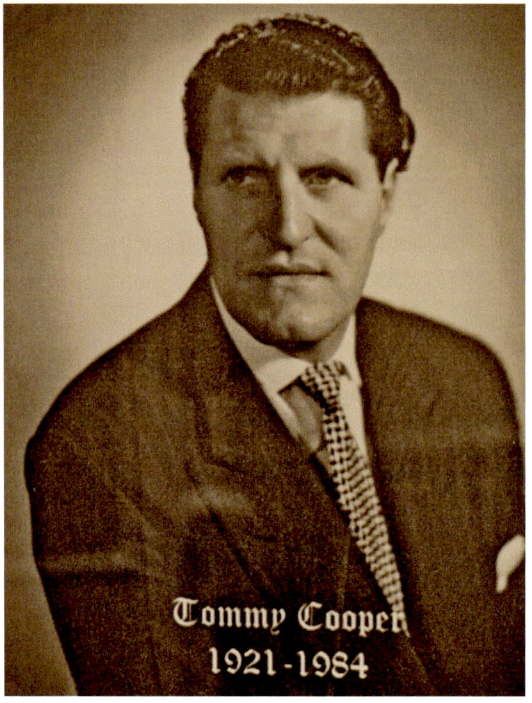

The walls of a ground-floor corridor are adorned with the Station Hotel's famous guests of the past, including Tommy Cooper, who was a regular performer at the Dudley Hippodrome.

participants reported feeling drained and exhausted after spending only brief periods there. One group fled in terror when one of the large light bulbs exploded, plunging them into darkness. Tales of dark, shadowy figures in a tunnel that linked the cellar to the Hippodrome have dwindled into mere rumours since it was sealed off sometime in the 1990s.

Eager to learn more about the hotel's ghostly history, I visited the hotel and requested their most haunted room. The receptionist handed me a key and directed me towards a grand staircase, adorned with a wine-coloured carpet that contrasted strikingly with the pristine white walls surrounding it. Ascending to the second floor, I arrived at the door of room 214. At first glance, there was nothing exceptional about this room; the walls, doors, and skirting boards matched the stark white sheets on the twin beds, which faced a small kitchenette on the opposite side. At the far end of the room sat two leather armchairs surrounding a tiny round table in front of the only window. However, many believe this nondescript room to be particularly haunted, a fact that Tony, the hotel's owner, was eager to mention when I encountered him in the restaurant later that evening.

When Tony took ownership of the hotel, all the rooms underwent modernisation and refurbishment. One morning, a contractor staying in the haunted room came rushing down the stairs, clutching his suitcase and complaining to the receptionist that his room was haunted. After enduring a night of inexplicable noises, the sight of a toilet roll unfurling from the bathroom into the bedroom proved to be his final straw. At least he remembered his suitcase. Other frightened guests have apparently refused to re-enter the room to retrieve their belongings. Some visitors reported glimpsing a faint figure standing by the window, while others have claimed to witness

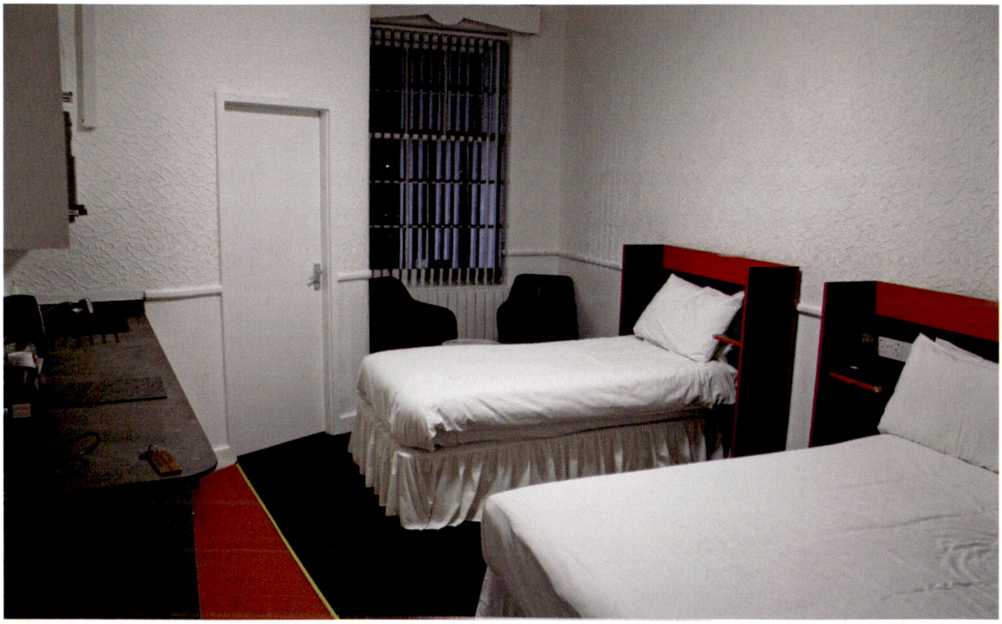

Room 214 is reputedly the most haunted room at the Station Hotel.

furniture moving on its own. A guest who stayed in 2014 alleged that upon waking, they found one of the beds positioned diagonally across the room. During my visit, Tony recounted the experience of a mother and daughter who spent the night there; the daughter claimed to have felt her arm being lifted by an invisible force during the night.

The spooky experiences aren't confined to this one room, as the adjacent rooms also have their fair share of haunts. For decorative purposes, an old-fashioned pram was placed by the window in room 217. One day, Tony was showing some people around the building and briefly went into the room, before locking up as he left. Shortly afterwards, on returning, he found the pram had moved in front of the door. Guests in room 216 have also reported seeing shadowy figures and the TV turning itself on, with the remote safely out of reach in a closed drawer. The corridor outside these rooms is renowned for the sound of children playing and laughing, most recently by staff member Charlotte, who heard the strange sounds first-hand while staying over with a friend on New Year's Eve.

Elsewhere in the hotel, the expansive stairwells have motion sensors that turn on the lights when guests walk up them; these have been known to illuminate even when no one is around as if an entity invisible to the human eye is ascending. Charlotte told me other colleagues in the kitchen area had also spotted dark figures.

If you're planning a stay in Dudley in the future but feeling nervous about what you will encounter at The Station Hotel, you may be reassured to know that I didn't come face to face with any of its spectral residents during my stay. However, the chilling tales and the hotel's eerie atmosphere made for an unforgettable night. It's not every day that you have the chance to sleep in a place steeped in history, mystery, and the unexplained.

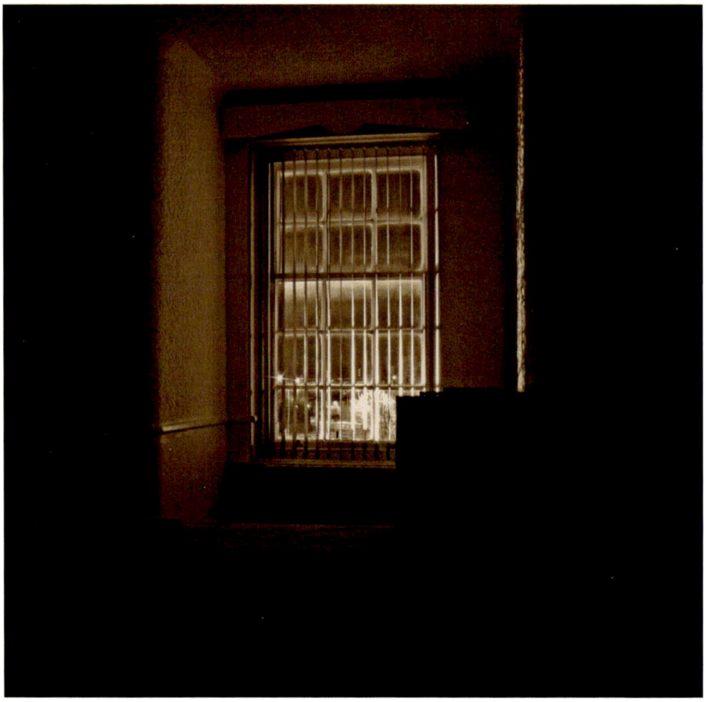

Some people have seen the faint outline of a person standing by the window in room 214.

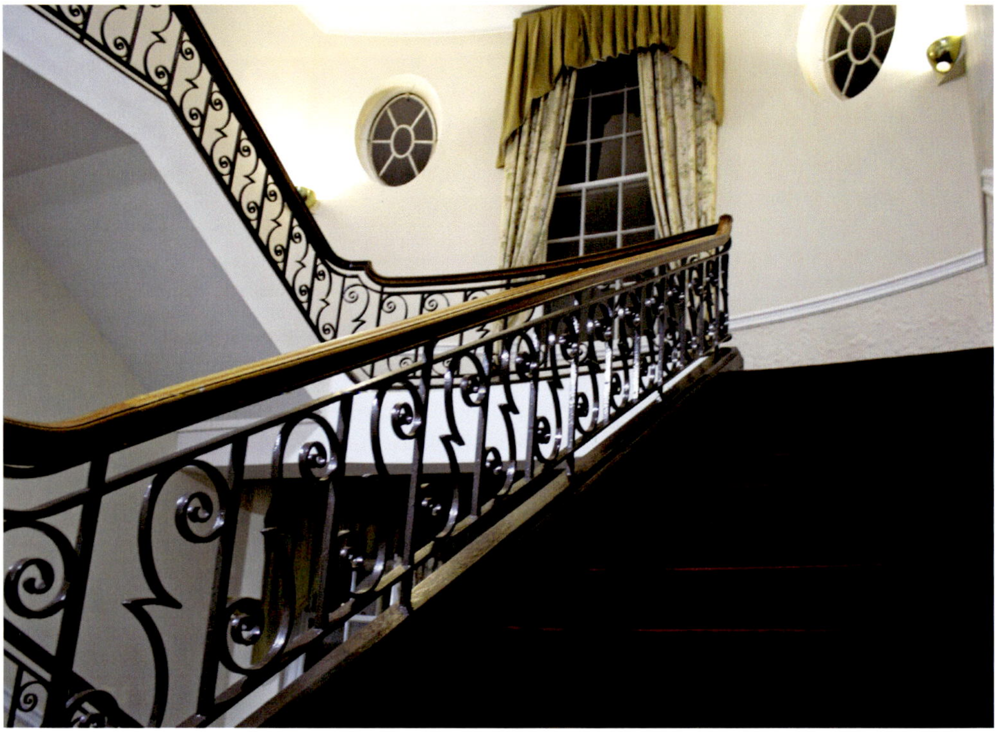

The grand staircase at the Station Hotel.

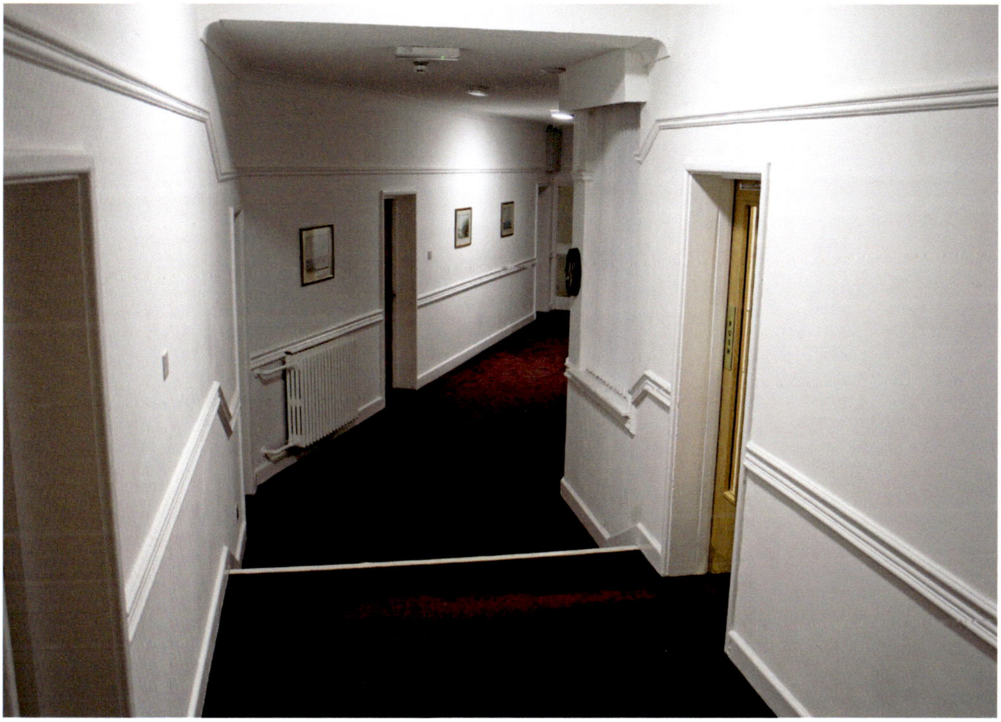

The corridors leading to and from the many rooms also have a haunted reputation, with the sounds of children laughing and playing heard by several guests.

Dudley Priory Ruins

Surrounded by modern-day housing estates, the ruins of St James Priory stand as a reminder of the area's religious past. Founded in 1160, it served as a place of work and worship for Cluniac monks, playing a pivotal role in the local communities. Centuries have elapsed since the last prayer was chanted within the priory walls, yet the stones seem to retain the memory of the monks' chorus. On the quietest of nights, a few fortunate individuals have reported hearing the angelic hum of their eternal hymn. Many claim to have seen the monks, robed in black, silently roaming between the crumbling walls and the surrounding grounds. These figures, with their large, heavy hoods concealing their faces, instil a sense of dread and unease in those who encounter them.

Ownership of the priory changed hands multiple times after its closure in 1539, under Henry VIII's Dissolution of the Monasteries. Initially granted to John Dudley, visible from his main residence at Dudley Castle, the priory's history took a dramatic turn. Following Henry VIII's death, Dudley led the government for young King Edward VI. However, after Edward's premature death aged fifteen, Dudley's attempt to place his daughter-in-law, Lady Jane Grey, on the throne led to his execution for high treason in August 1553. Subsequently, Dudley Priory lay abandoned for a long period, falling into disrepair. During the Industrial Revolution, locals repurposed it for various manufacturing activities.

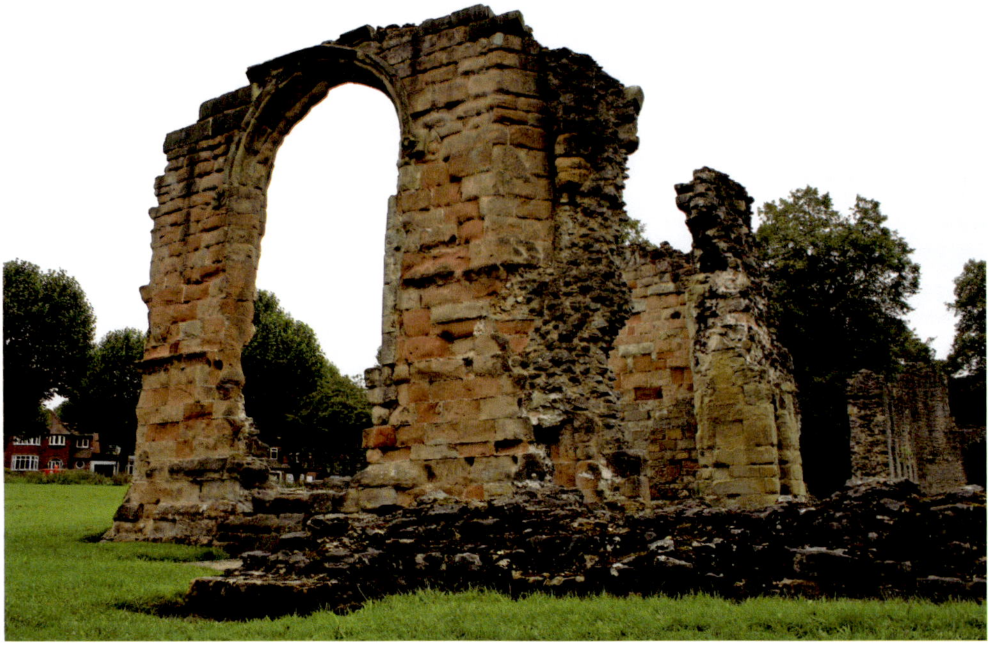

The church section of the priory ruins forms the most intact part of the remaining structure.

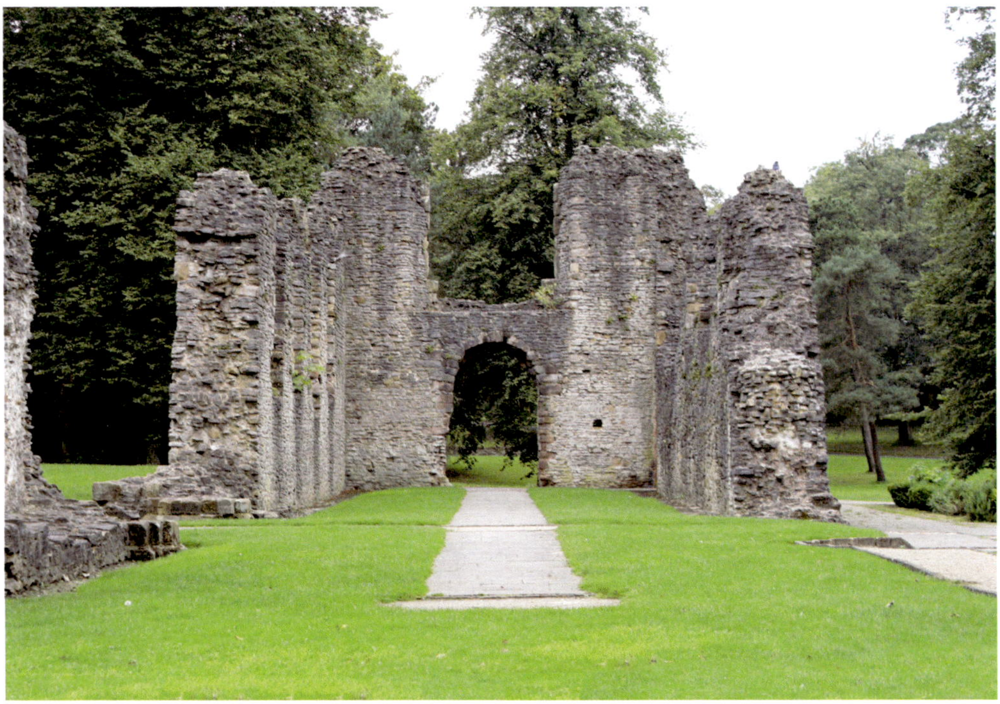

Looking from the chancel, from where an altar would have once stood, towards the church's main entrance.

Today, the priory's few remaining walls stand in a parkland, frequented by dog walkers and cyclists. However, they do not walk its paths alone, as the park is said to be haunted by the apparition of a 'white lady'. According to one account, a group visiting the ruins at night encountered an extremely pale, middle-aged woman dressed in white, wailing behind a tree. Her cold, piercing stare and skeletal face terrified one of the group members, prompting a hasty retreat.

While such vivid encounters are rare, many believe spirits can make their presence known through other means, including smell. In the late 1950s, seventeen-year-old Ernie Marson and his friend Tex experienced an unexplainable odour near the priory, and shared his story with the *Black Country Bugle* in October 1999.

As the teenagers walked near Bluebell Park, a loud, animal-like scream emanating from the trees halted them. Intrigued and slightly apprehensive, they paused to listen. When the scream echoed a second time, curiosity overcame their fear, and they decided to investigate. Venturing deeper into the woods, they noticed an eerie stillness settling around them, the dense canopy obscuring the last remnants of the evening's light. A few hundred yards in, they abruptly stopped. Although they saw nothing unusual, an overpowering stench, akin to a dog in desperate need of a bath, assaulted their senses. It seemed to have a life of its own, first enveloping Tex before shifting towards Ernie. Overwhelmed by the foul odour and its mysterious movement, the boys quickly retreated to the safety of the main road. After a restless night, riddled with doubts about their experience, they decided to return to the same spot the following night.

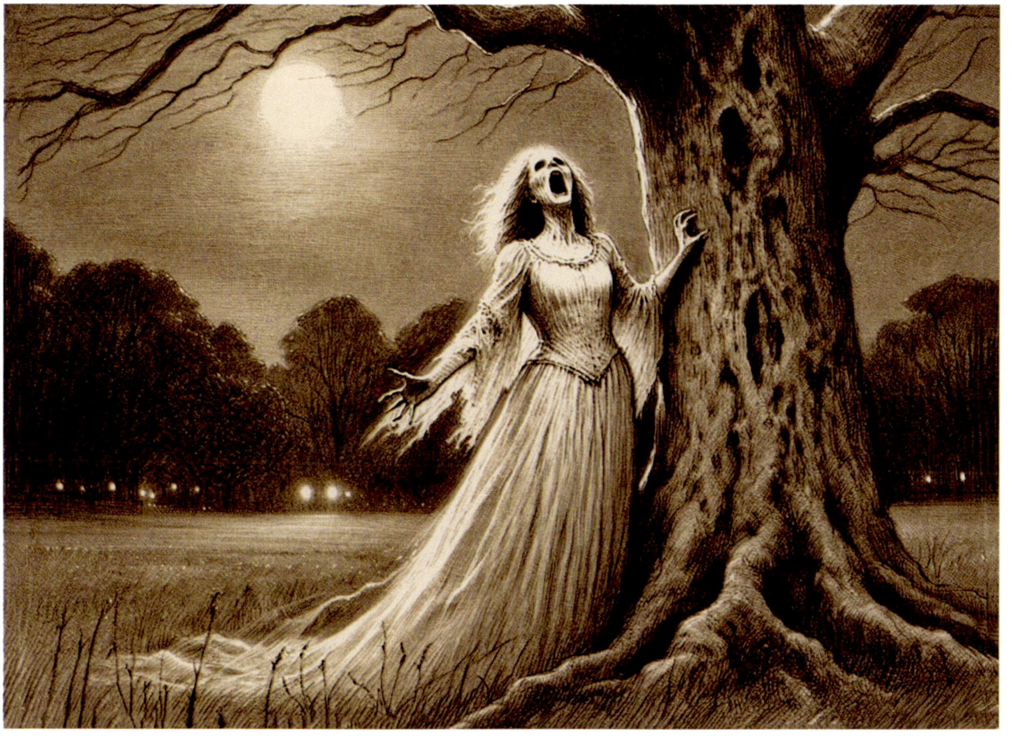

The vision of a wailing ghost in the Dudley Priory parkland would be enough to send anyone fleeing.

Perhaps, they thought, it was all a figment of their imagination. However, twenty-four hours later, as they stepped off the main road into the dark woods, the same putrid smell greeted them, moving eerily around them once again.

The next night, at the Savoy in Castle Hill, they shared their bizarre encounters with friends. Met with laughter and scepticism, their friends playfully suggested a group visit to Bluebell Park the following night. They agreed, but this time the mysterious smell was absent. Embarrassed and unable to explain the previous night's events, Ernie and his friend chose not to explore further.

Years later, in his fifties, Ernie began a new job working with the elderly. Among them was an eighty-four-year-old woman named Margaret, nearing the end of her life, and eager to share tales from her days in the Black Country. One morning, she recounted the history of Dudley Priory. 'It was burned down, you know,' said Margaret, 'It was burned down, and it was a terrible sin. Lots of young nuns were burned with it. And, on the Priory Estate, those girls still walk today.' She leaned forward, grabbed Ernie's hand, and gave it a squeeze. 'Oh, you'll never see them,' she said, tightening her grip on his hand, 'but if one of them ever walks past you, by God, you'll smell her!'

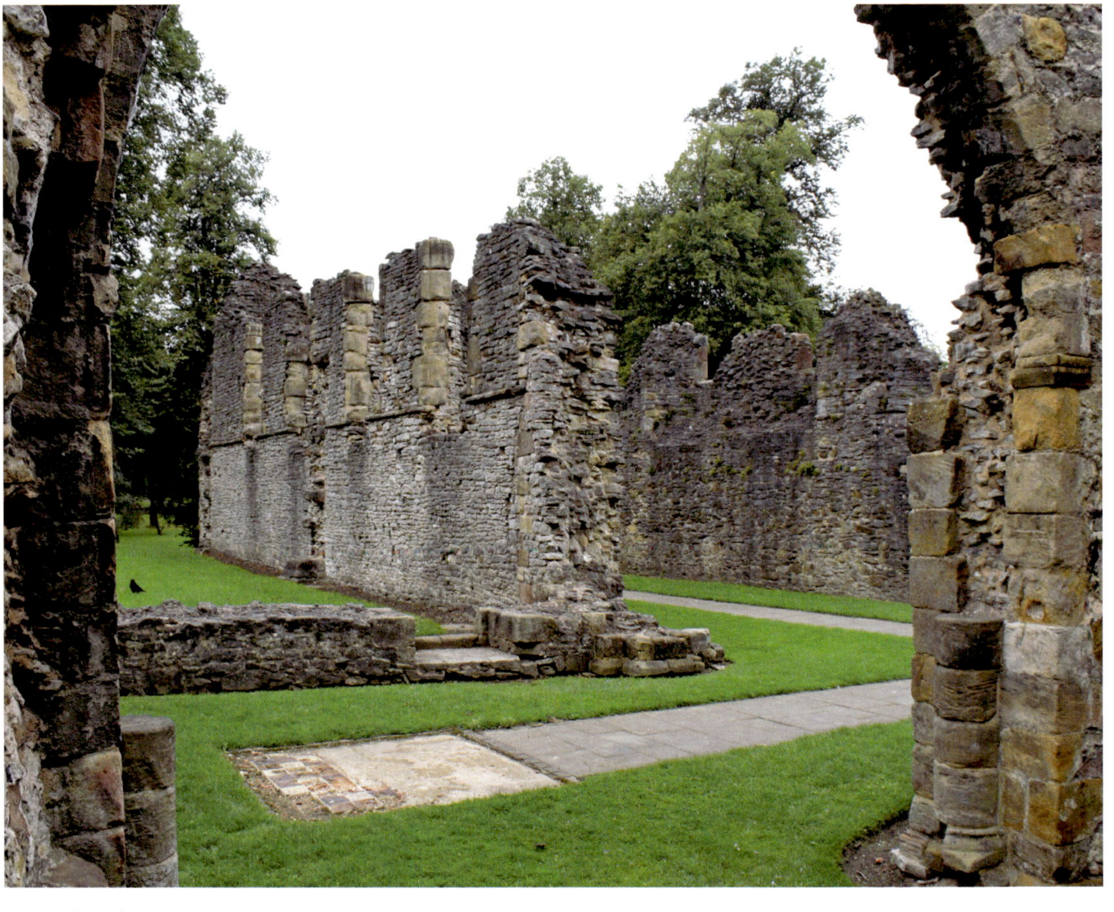

The chapel, Dudley Priory.

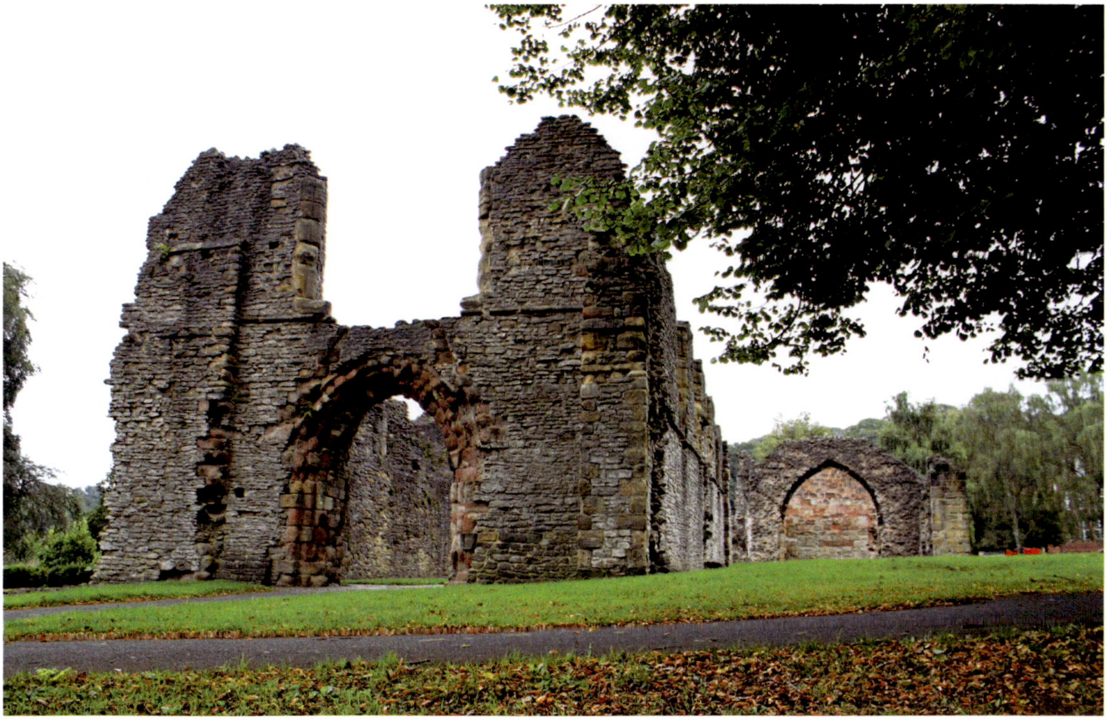

The church entrance, with the adjoining chapel to the right, looking towards Dudley Castle.

Himley Hall

As the English Civil War raged into its third year, by 1645, King Charles I was losing. Following a brutal series of battles, his forces were thinning, leaving him with little option but to retreat and regroup, lest he suffer inevitable defeat at the muskets of the pursuing Parliamentarians. On 15 May, the King and his army took refuge at Himley Hall, home to the staunchly royalist Lords of Dudley. He was safe from Parliamentarians, but not from betrayal within his own ranks. Richard Symonds, a diarist of the Civil War, chronicled a grim event during this stay. A soldier, accused of mutiny, was hanged on the estate and buried in its grounds on 16 May 1645. Yet, his death did not end his presence at Himley Hall. Dressed in Cavalier uniform, his restless spirit is said to roam the hall's grounds. Local fishermen have reported seeing an 'old-fashioned soldier' silently moving through the trees near the large pool on at least three occasions. The apparition has also been sighted on the roads encircling the park, where one startled witness reported a figure darting in front of her car, identifiable by its long Cavalier-style boots.

The vast pool within Himley Hall's grounds, a popular spot for anglers, has its own mysterious tales. These early risers often share stories of a mysterious young lady, wearing a long, antiquated dress, walking the grounds at dawn. In July 2010, Stanley Gresswell, an avid fisherman, arrived at the pool around 7 a.m. Despite the summer month, the dawn air was crisp, and a delicate mist rose over the water's surface.

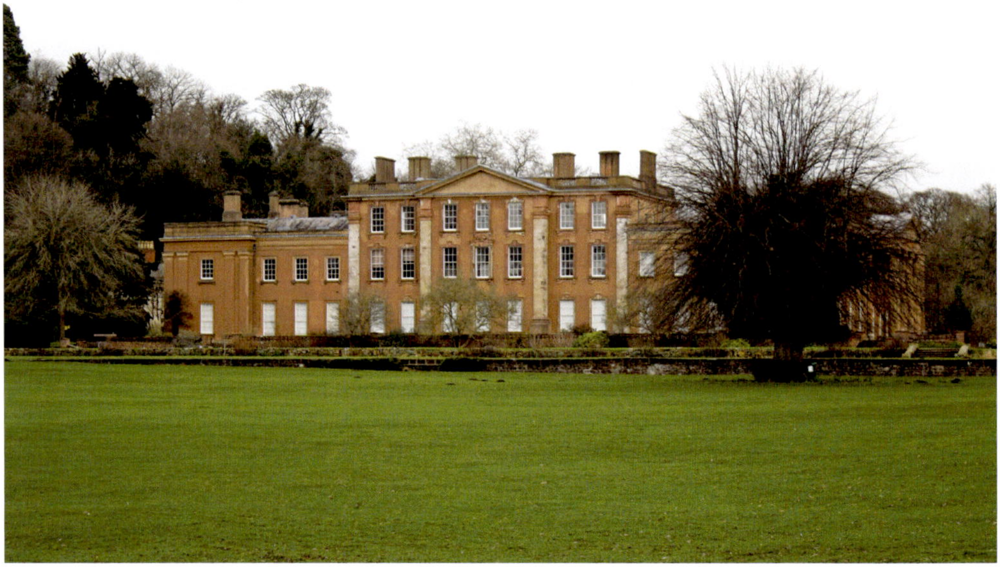

Himley Hall, built in the eighteenth century, became the home of the Lords of Dudley after the great fire at Dudley Castle.

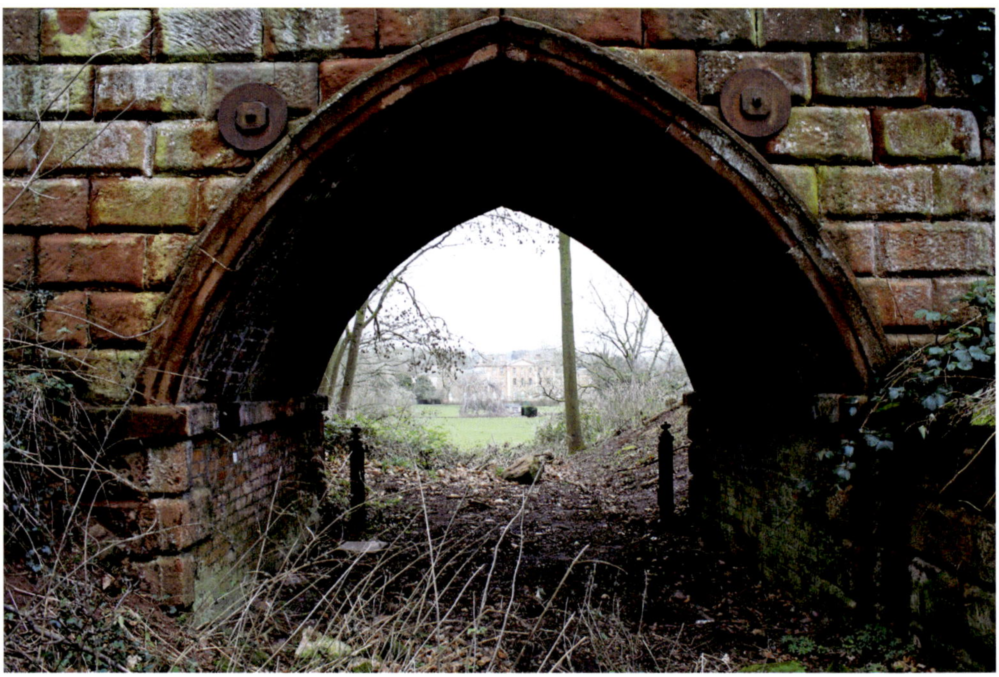

The hall overlooks an impressive 180-acre parkland created by Lancelot 'Capability' Brown, a famous landscape gardener who designed the parklands for around 170 stately residences, including Belvoir Castle and Blenheim Palace.

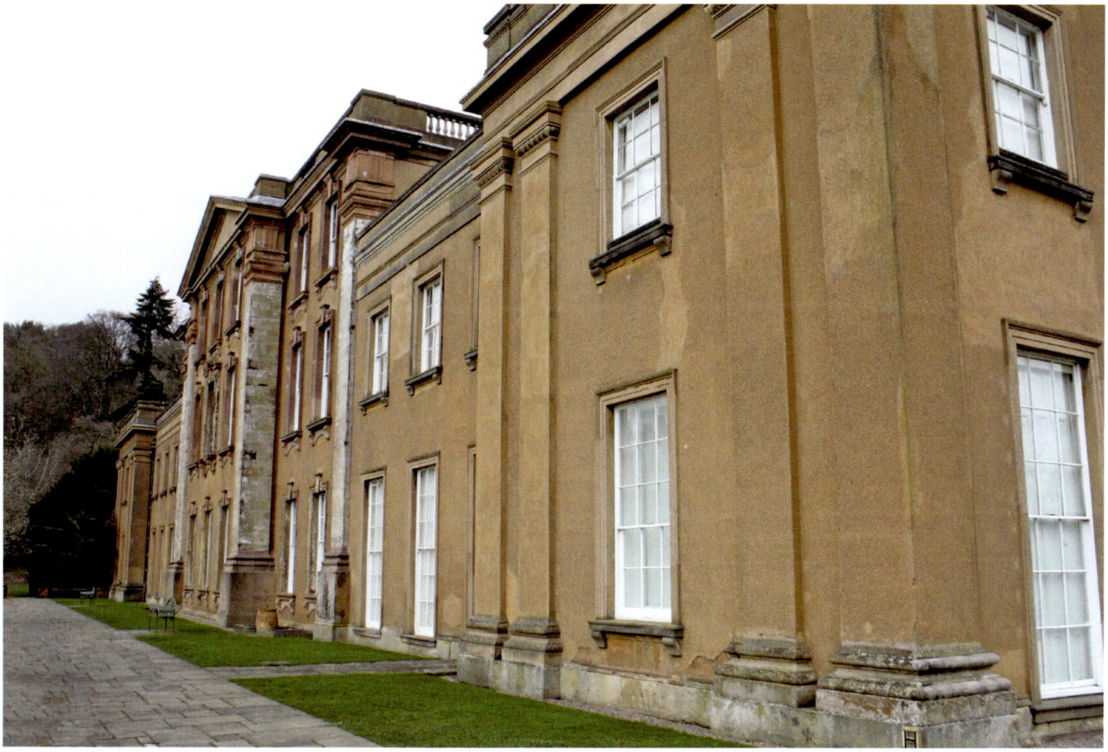

While the hall isn't known for hauntings, its grounds are home to several ghosts.

As Stanley prepared his fishing gear, he noticed a young woman in a long gown wandering near the hall. Minding his own business, Stanley continued readying his fishing equipment and paid little attention to the out-of-place lady. He occasionally glanced in her direction and watched as she drifted towards the hall and eventually out of sight behind an old, strange-looking tree. Shortly afterwards, a warden overseeing the hall and its grounds emerged from the building and approached the fishing pond. Curiosity gnawing at him, Stanley asked the warden if he knew who the oddly dressed woman was. The warden, surprised, informed him that no one should have been there at that hour, hinting that Stanley might have witnessed one of Himley Hall's famed ghosts. 'I don't believe in ghosts,' insists Stanley. 'Even now, I am still a non-believer, but I can't explain what I saw that morning.'

However, these apparitions aren't confined to the pool area. Former wardens of Himley Hall have confirmed sightings of a spectral figure in a long dress on the roads encircling the 180-acre parkland, causing near-misses for motorists, at least five times over a nineteen-year period. The ghost is described as a young woman, adorned in a floor-length, dark grey dress, appearing to be of Victorian style. Each encounter involves her running away from the hall at a considerable speed, vanishing when concerned motorists stop to check, leaving them feeling shaken and confused. Her apparition is believed to be a senior servant girl from the times when Himley Hall was the residence of the Lords of Dudley, who made it their principal home after Dudley Castle was ravaged by a catastrophic fire. What she is running from, we'll never know.

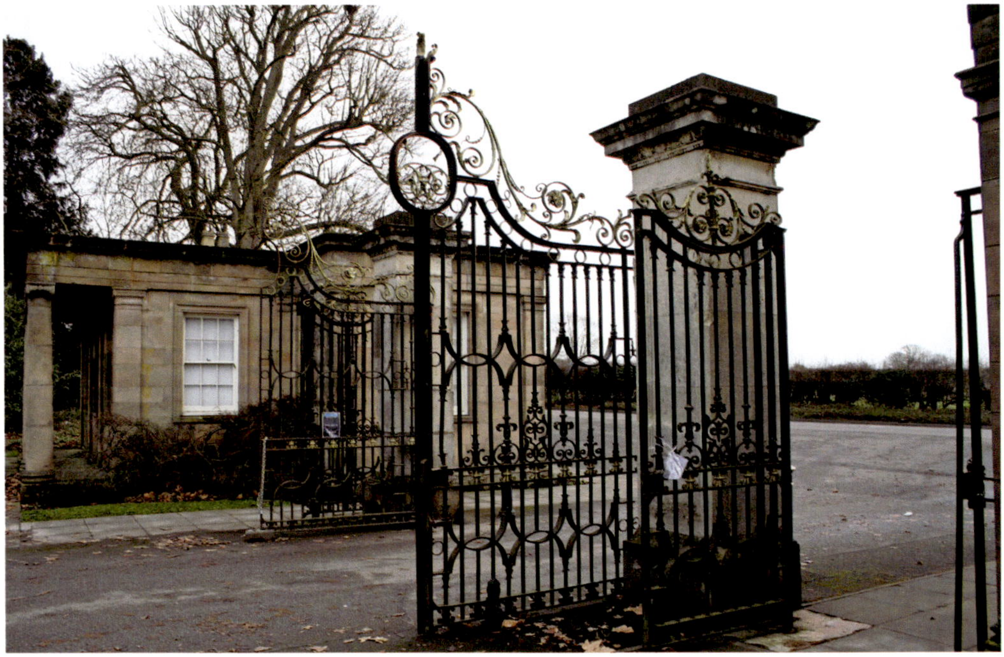

The main gates at Himley Hall.

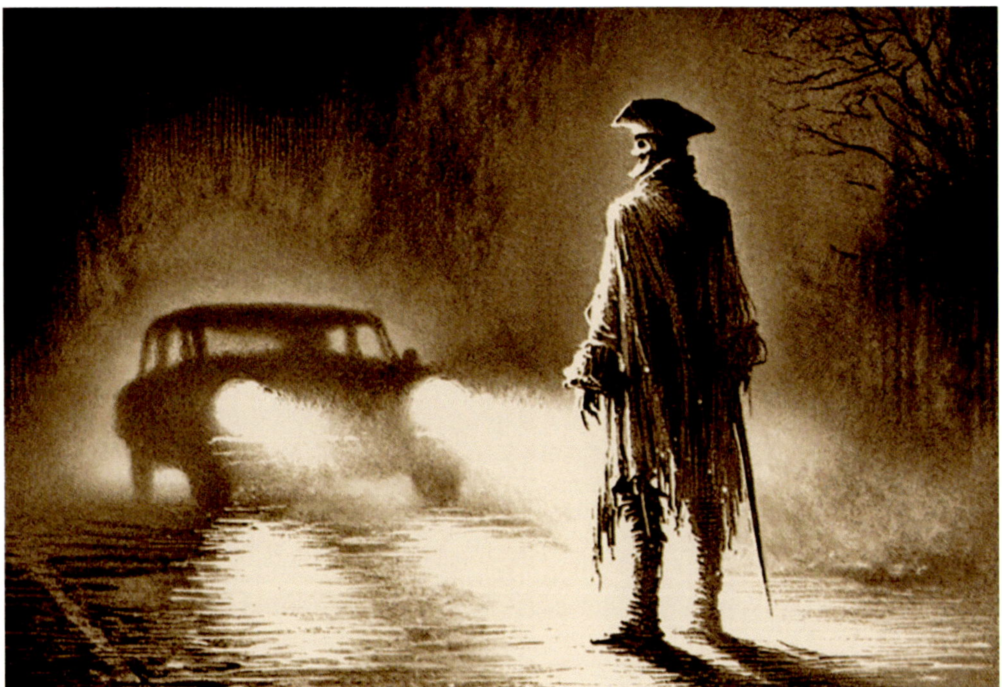

The roads surrounding the hall and its parklands have been the scene of many near-misses with phantom soldiers and former housemaids in old-fashioned clothing.

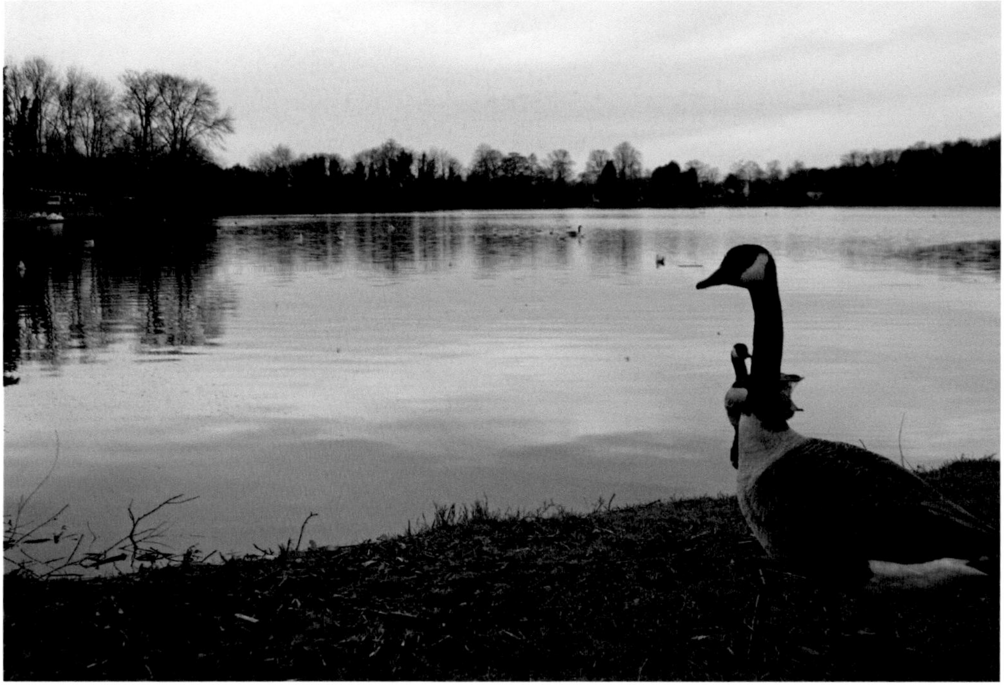

At the far end of the parkland is a large pool frequented by fishermen, many of whom have seen the ghost of a young woman in a long gown.

Holbeche House and Gideon Grove

From the stillness of daybreak, an almighty explosion boomed across Himley and the surrounding villages. For Richard Walsh, the Sheriff of Worcestershire, and his posse of armed men, it was a beacon leading them straight to their prey: the conspirators behind the Gunpowder Plot.

Three days earlier, on 5 November 1605, the ill-fated attempt to blow up the House of Lords and kill Protestant King James I was foiled. Guy Fawkes and the men guarding thirty-six barrels of gunpowder beneath the house were arrested, but the masterminds behind the plot escaped and fled north. During their retreat, they stole weapons from Warwick Castle and took gunpowder from Hewell Grange near Redditch, triggering an arrest warrant that the Sheriff was eager to fulfil.

A plume of black smoke rising above the trees led the men to their final destination, Holbeche House, a mansion owned by one of the plot leaders' associates. They arrived at a scene of devastation: the floor was littered with parts of what was once a sitting room, now a smouldering pile of rubble. On their journey to the house, the plotters were forced to cross a river, soaking their gunpowder stash. Their attempts to dry it by an open fire, where stray sparks are inevitable, led to a detonation that would be their undoing.

Knowing the conspirators might still be sheltering inside, the Sheriff read out his warrant and ordered the men to surrender. In response, musket shots began to fire their way from behind the burning timbers. The surviving plotters were not planning to go down without a fight. A chaotic gun battle ensued, leaving scars on the hall's timbers that are still visible today. Matchlocks fired furiously from both sides, but the plotters, heavily outnumbered, eventually succumbed to the might of the posse. After the melee, as one of the Sheriff's men was walking amongst the lifeless bodies strewn upon the smoking rubble, he noticed a survivor attempting to escape on horseback. The man, wearing a dark velvet coat and a tricorn hat, bolted toward Wombourne Common. In a matter of moments, a few of the Sheriff's men mounted their horses and pursued. They caught their target quickly; the young man and his horse had careered into a deep bog, becoming stuck. The young escapee pleaded for a rope, but instead, the posse raised their matchlocks and fired several shots into his chest.

Leaving their target to descend into his murky grave, the men returned to Holbeche House, where golden embers and ash still rained down upon their tricorns. There, they learned that all of the conspirators had been killed or captured, apart from two who fled on horseback in the opposite direction. The man they killed was not involved in the plot. He was Gideon Grove, a young groom who worked for the master of the house, an innocent man who paid with his life.

Centuries later, several people claim to have heard the sounds of galloping horses on Bridgnorth Road in Wombourne, near the site of this unlawful killing. Others speak of a dark rider, seen thundering through the surrounding lanes, and trampling crops in wheatfields, while some claim to have seen the body of young Gideon rising from the swamp where legend states he met his untimely death. On 13 July 1971, Joe Green, a local Coach and Travel Proprietor, was motoring home around 11.20 p.m. on Bridgnorth Road. Describing himself as someone who has never believed in ghosts

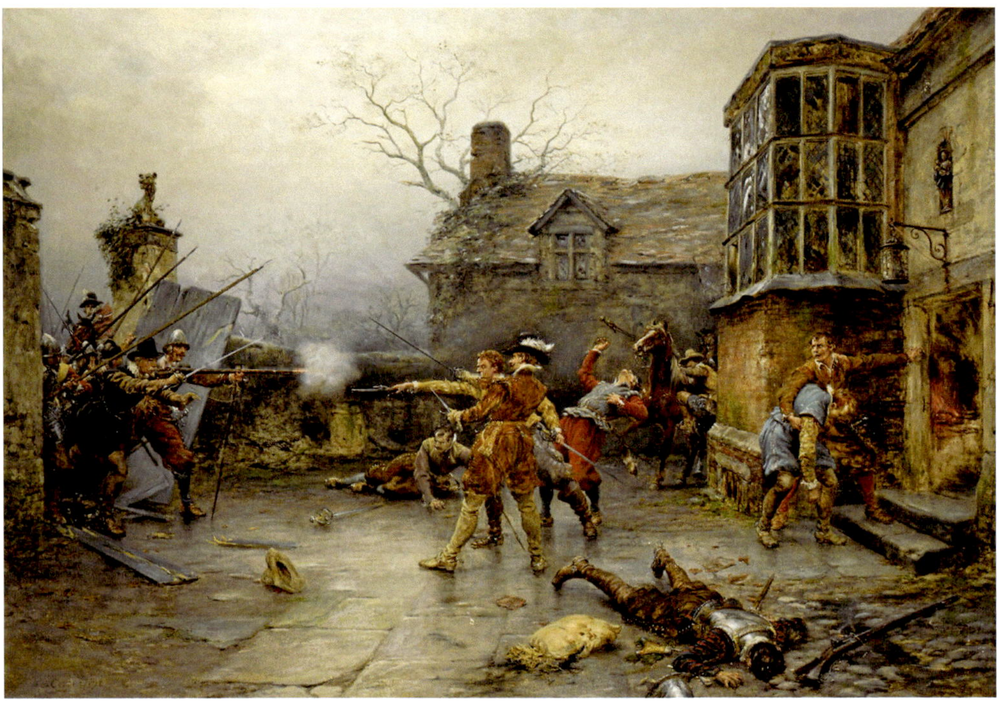

The Gunpowder Plot: the conspirators' last stand at Holbeche House. (Alamy; E. Crofts 1892)

and is as down-to-earth as they come, he experienced something he could not explain. On a well-lit stretch of road between the Brick Bridge pub and the Common Road junction, the lights overhead suddenly went out. Mr Green stopped and got out of his car, hearing the thudding of hoofbeats and seeing a rider approaching, travelling around 3 feet above the road surface. The rider, dressed in black thigh-length riding boots, a dark blue velvet coat, and a cocked hat, galloped past at tremendous speed, appearing to be fleeing from someone or something. As the rider passed, the trees behind lit up with a fiery glow in the direction of Holbeche House. Suddenly, the street lights came back on, and both the rider and the ominous glow behind him disappeared. A perplexed Mr Green returned home, sharing his story with friends and family. The vision remained a mystery until he read about the legend of Gideon Grove

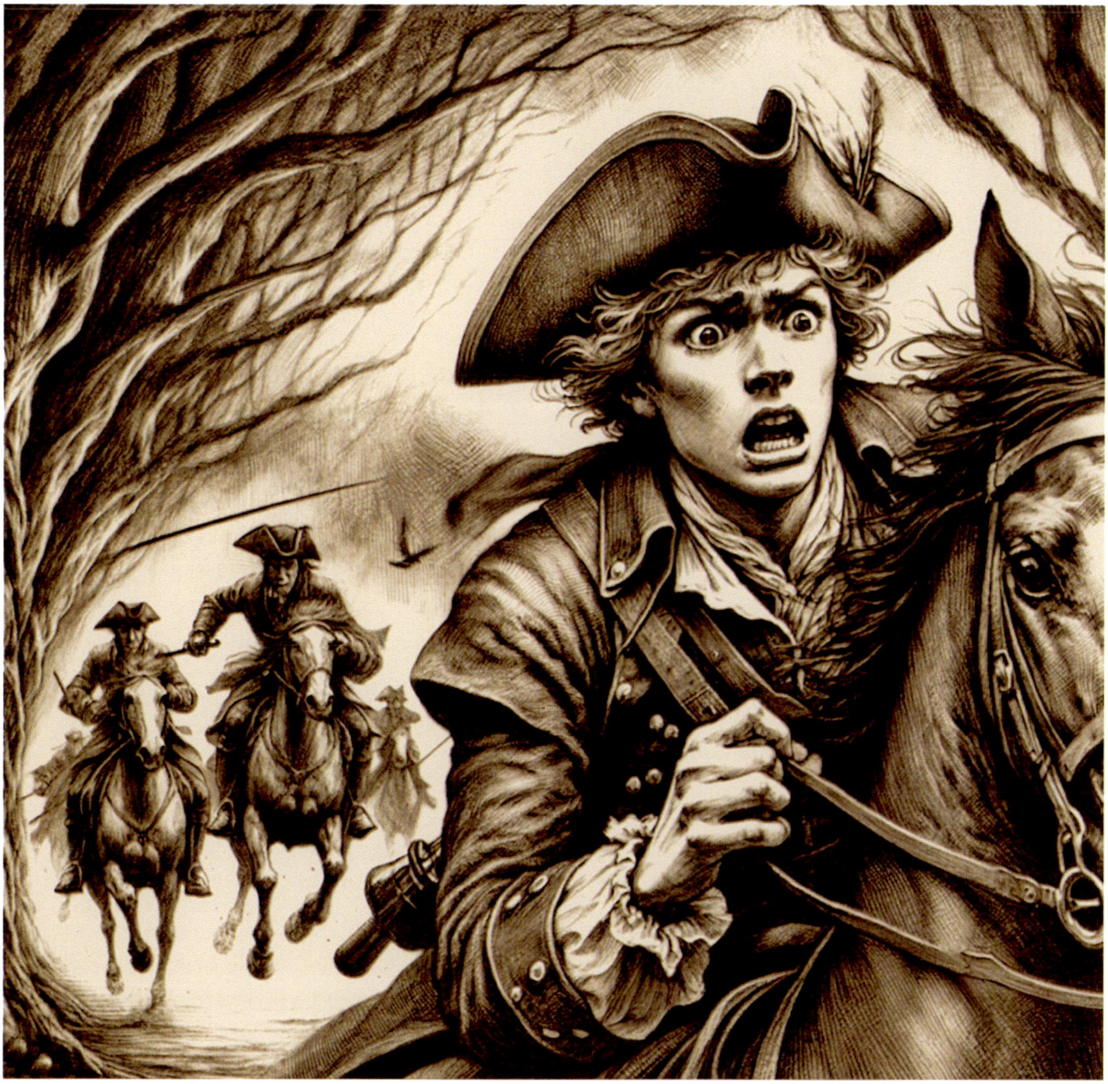

A case of mistaken identity, Gideon Grove flees the Sheriff's men towards his untimely death.

in the *Black Country Bugle* two years later. He had witnessed a scene, a time-slip, that occurred some 350 years earlier.

Monica Bowen also recounted her experience to the *Black Country Bugle*. Her sighting was on Bridgnorth Road, around half a mile further from Himley than Mr Green's. It was around 2.30 a.m. on 1 August 1973 when Monica was riding on the back of a friend's motorcycle, returning home from a social evening at Ditton Priors. Approaching a crossroads near Wombourne, the motorcycle's engine suddenly stalled. Moments later, after a stillness that charged the air with terror, the deafening sound of thudding hoofbeats surrounded them, though no riders were visible. Unaware of the legend, Monica shared her experience the following day with a colleague, who informed her of the phantom horseman.

What makes these tales all the more sinister is the discovery of human remains in a small area of woodland on the side of Bridgnorth Road. Some believed the remains belonged to a local elderly tramp; others said they belonged to the phantom rider who had spooked locals for centuries.

According to Sheriff Walsh's account, some of the men fled by the time they caught up with the retinue at Holbeche, but others, ignoring the Sheriff's warnings to come quietly, hunkered down to fight. There was no mention of Gideon, nor even the master of the house. However, intrigued by the legend, local metal detectorists went to the swamp and found a musket ball on the swamp's edge. A few feet away, they also found an old pistol ball and a large pewter button.

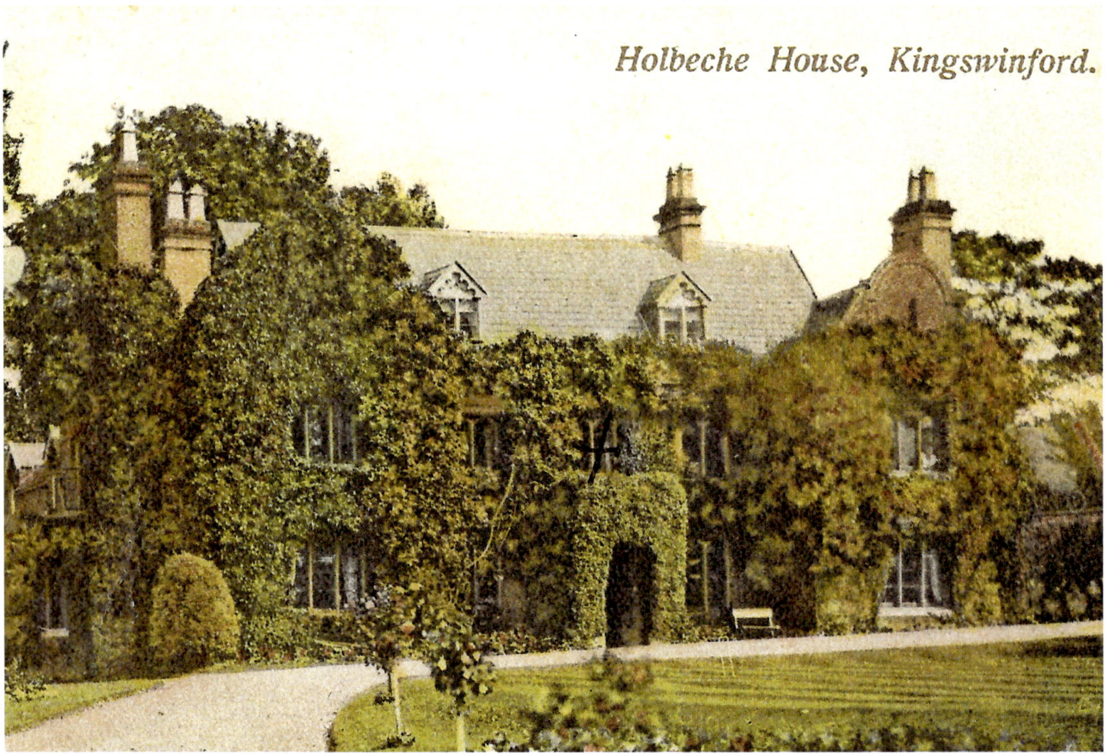

Holbeche House is abandoned and in a state of disrepair today. This postcard, sent to an address in Germany in 1917, is a more attractive representation of the grand house.

The Crooked House

While the tale of Gideon Grove's unjust killing could just be a myth, the story behind the unlawful demise of one of the Black Country's most cherished buildings is all too real for many locals to bear. When I first contemplated creating this book, I was undecided about including the Crooked House pub among the many stories. However, on the evening of 5 August 2023, during the book's development, the iconic structure was gutted by a fire, almost certainly caused by arson. Two days later, the charred remains were illegally demolished using a hired excavator, eliminating any chance of investigation or restoration. While Gideon Grove's killers would have gone unpunished, those responsible for the destruction of 'Britain's wonkiest pub' are likely to face charges for its unlawful demolition. Sadly, that won't bring back the iconic building or its resident ghosts.

Constructed in 1765, the building initially stood as an unremarkable farmhouse, similar to many others in the area at that time. In the early 1800s, however, mining works in the earth beneath the building caused one side to sink into the ground by approximately 4 feet. The resulting 15-degree tilt created optical illusions for those inside, where marbles appeared to roll uphill, and visitors felt unsteady on their feet without even a sip of alcohol. It was converted into a pub in 1830 and named the

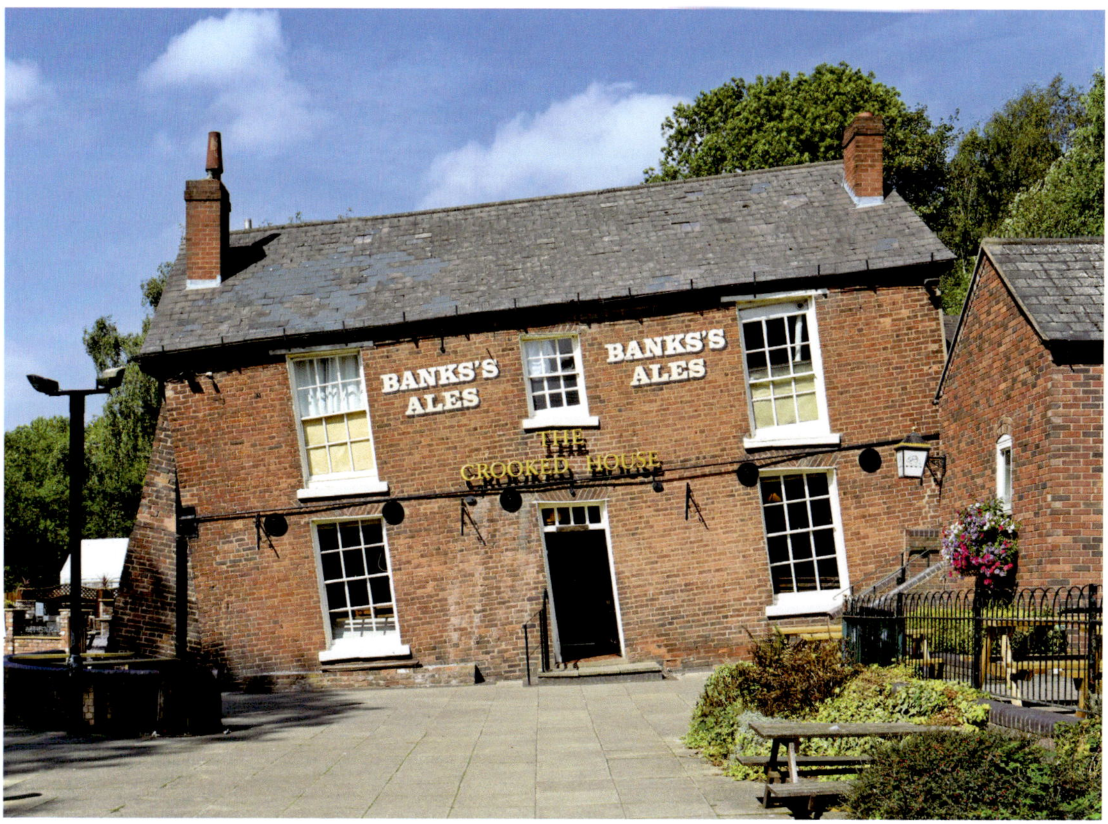

The Crooked House with its distinctive 15-degree tilt, and the buttresses to its left to prevent it from leaning further. (Courtesy of Andrew Homer)

Glynne Arms, in honour of its original owner, Sir Stephen Glynne. Glynne, responsible for much of the mining in the area, was also the brother-in-law of Prime Minister Gladstone. For many years, it was nicknamed Siden House, meaning Crooked House in the Black Country dialect, before being officially renamed as such in 2002. The building nearly met its end several times in the past, including in the 1940s when it became derelict and was condemned, and by a fire in 1986. On both occasions, it was saved only by vast sums of money, managing to survive until very recently.

The 2023 fire that led to the Crooked House's final demise sparked nationwide outrage, particularly among Black Country residents who reminisced about their visits to the much-loved pub. Amid their outpouring of memories, many spoke about encounters with the ghosts reputedly haunting the pub. The most famous is Polly, although she may actually be two separate ghosts. Some describe her as a young girl in a parlour maid's attire, often seen near the old fireplace, possibly harking back to the building's farmhouse days. Others believe Polly was a former barmaid, seen pouring a drink in the bar area. In both accounts, she vanished when anyone tried to get a closer look. She was also frequently blamed for odd occurrences in the bathrooms, such as hand dryers activating on their own and door handles rattling furiously, startling patrons and staff alike. Following the fire, many locals spoke about strange happenings in the bathrooms. One individual on social media recalled a childhood experience of cubicle doors slamming shut while she was alone in the toilets. In another incident,

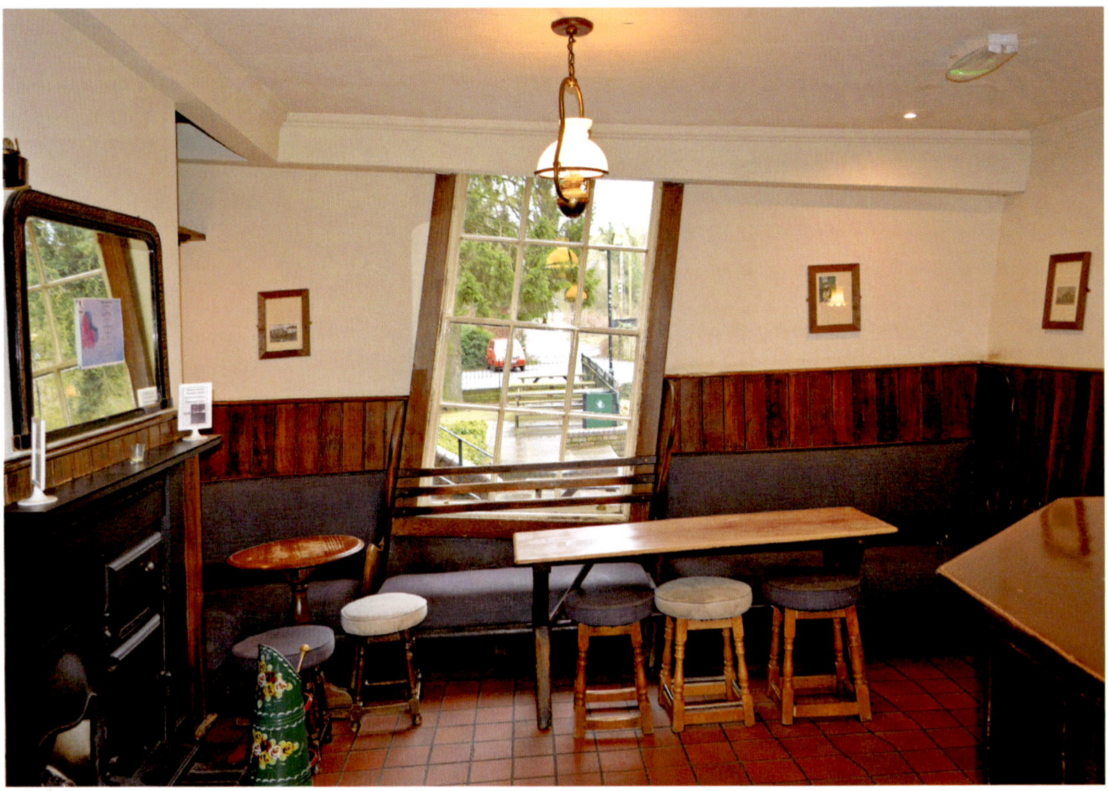

Inside the Crooked House, where you could be forgiven for thinking you've had a few too many drinks when sober. (Courtesy of Andrew Homer)

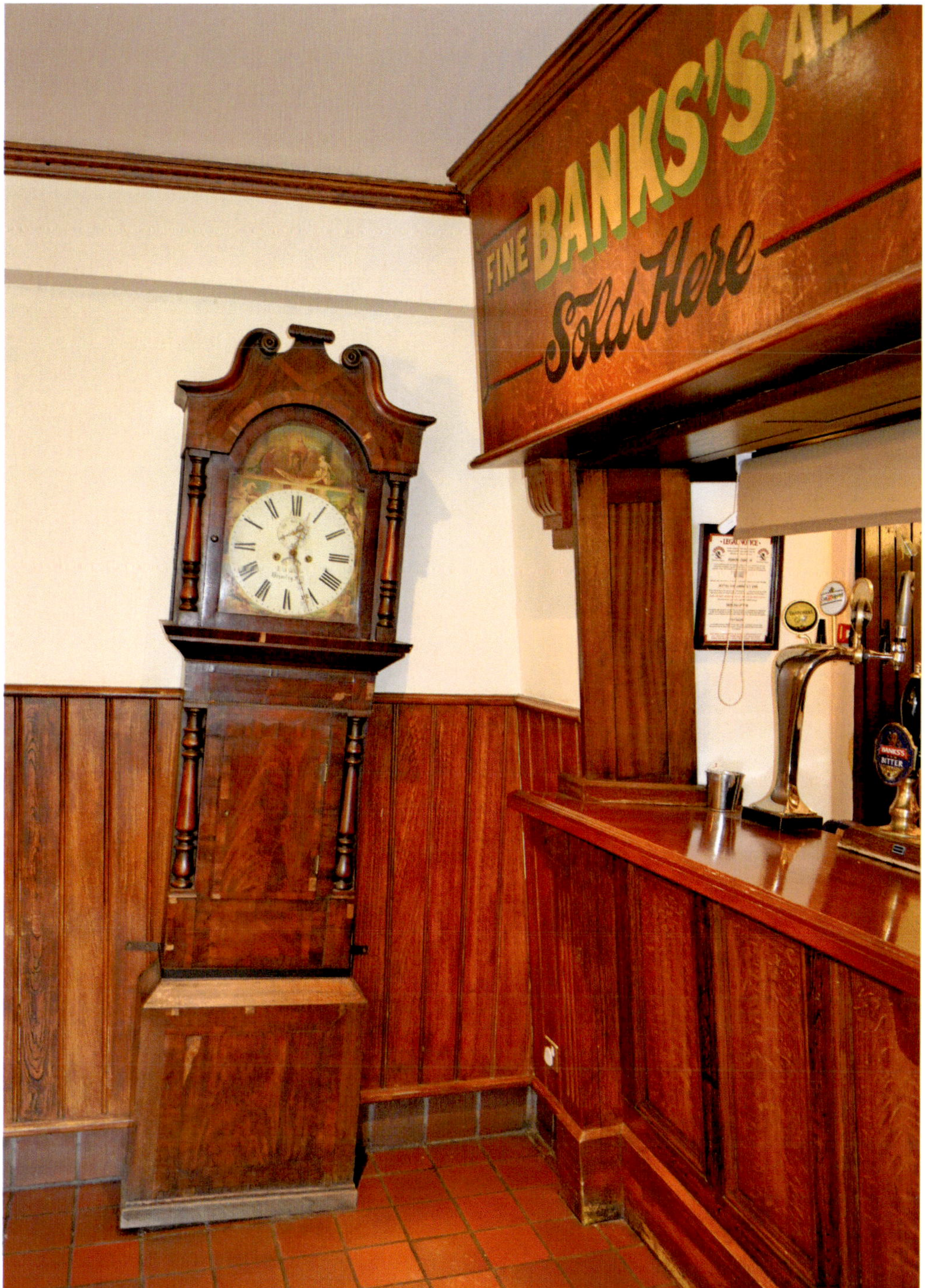

Inside the Crooked House. At the time of writing, the grandfather clock's whereabouts are a mystery that locals are eager to solve. (Courtesy of Andrew Homer)

a woman felt the air turn icy cold around her in the cubicle, followed by the distinct sound of a child singing nursery rhymes. These stories have led many to speculate that the ghost in the toilets might be that of a young girl instead.

Even non-believers like former landlord David Shotton couldn't help but find the Crooked House to be eerie. 'Table ninety-nine in the restaurant was always used by staff for end-of-night drinks after closing,' said David. He had just finished locking up and was helping the staff to clean the cutlery, which was always the last job of the night. They were chatting away, 'bantering between us all', David said, 'And then we heard the footsteps of a woman in what sounded like high heels coming from the

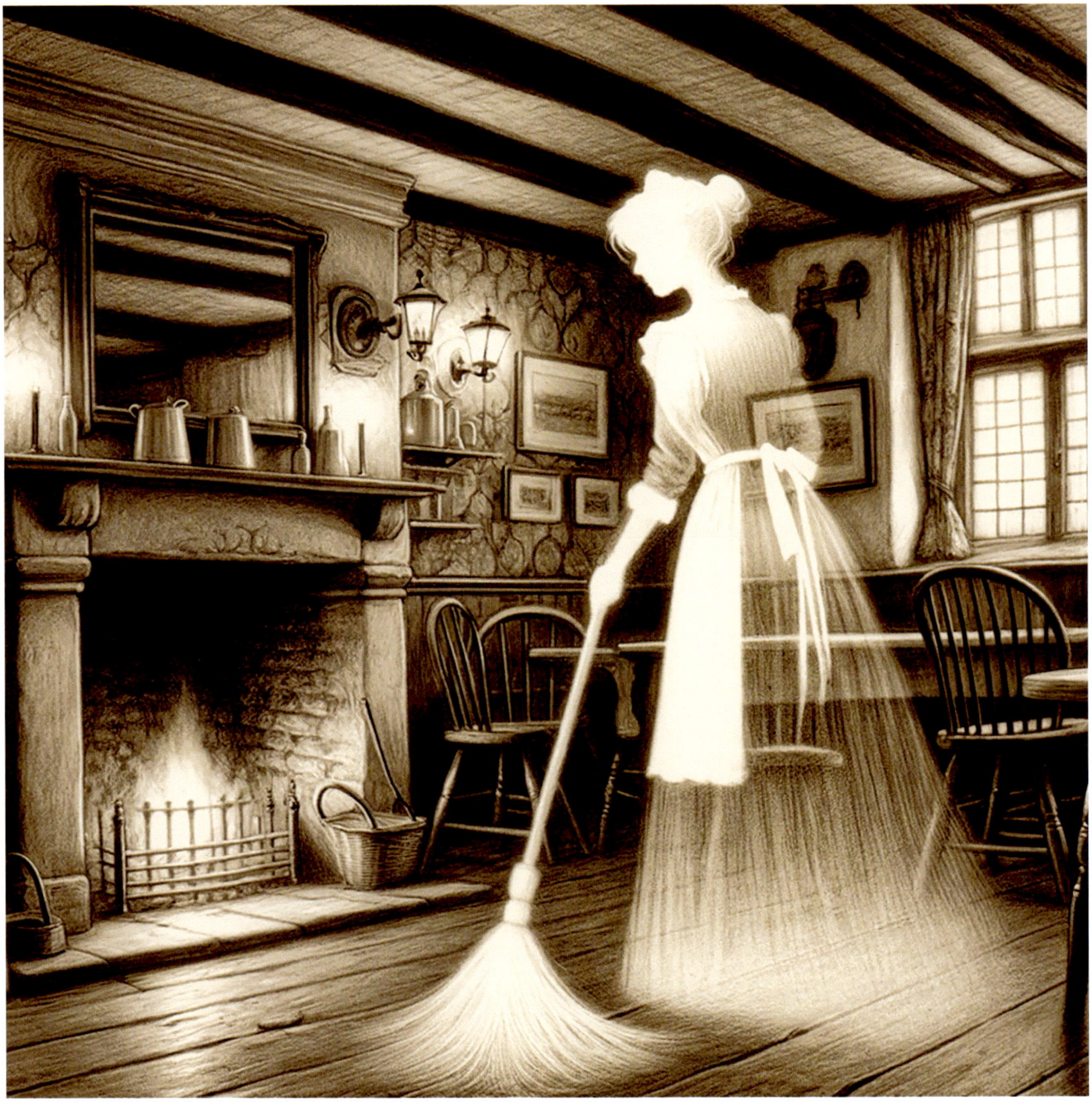

Polly was one of the pub's most famous ghosts, but the diversity of her sightings suggests more than one young woman haunted it.

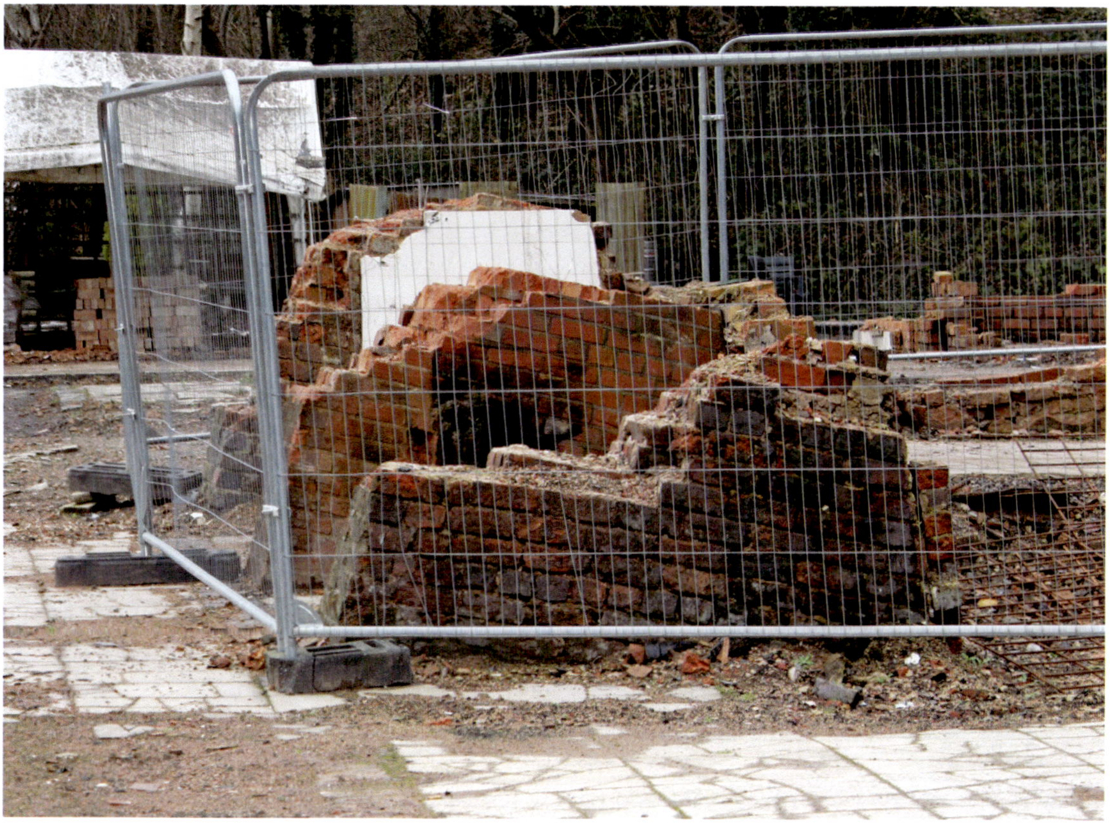

Visiting the site in late 2023, when only a few traces of the once-popular pub remain. The mighty buttresses that once supported the Crooked House are sinking into the collapsed cellar space beneath.

toilets and going into the lounge.' They loudly said the front door was locked, so to come the restaurant way in, but no one entered the room. Baffled, they went to see who it was, but there was no one in sight.

Another well-known Crooked House ghost is that of an elderly man, presumed by many to be a former landlord. Witnesses often saw him enter the old bar area, only to vanish before they could serve him. 'Loads of staff went to serve him,' a former landlord said, 'but he was never there.'

Photos of the Crooked House taken during the devastating fire seemed to some viewers to show the outlines of two spectres illuminated by the flames. While likely nothing more than an optical illusion, it's hard not to envision the spirits watching helplessly as their centuries-old home burned away, lost forever.

Kinver

The quaint village of Kinver, situated near the convergence of the Staffordshire, Shropshire, and Worcestershire counties, lies on the southern tip of what many consider either just inside or out of the Black Country. Its history dates back to the

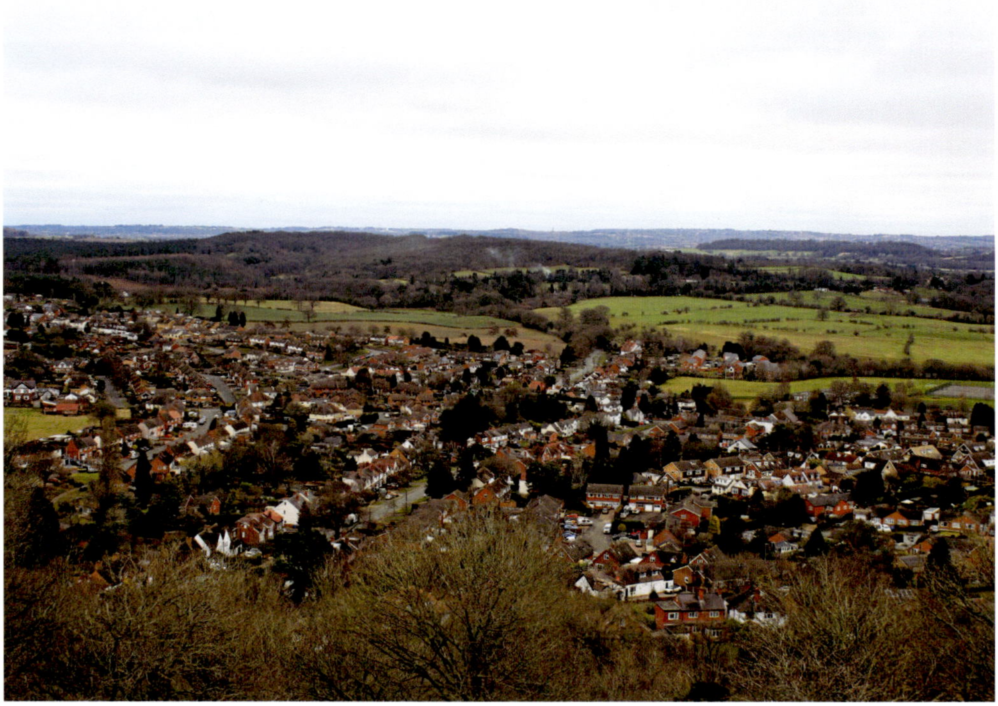

Kinver, viewed from Kinver Edge.

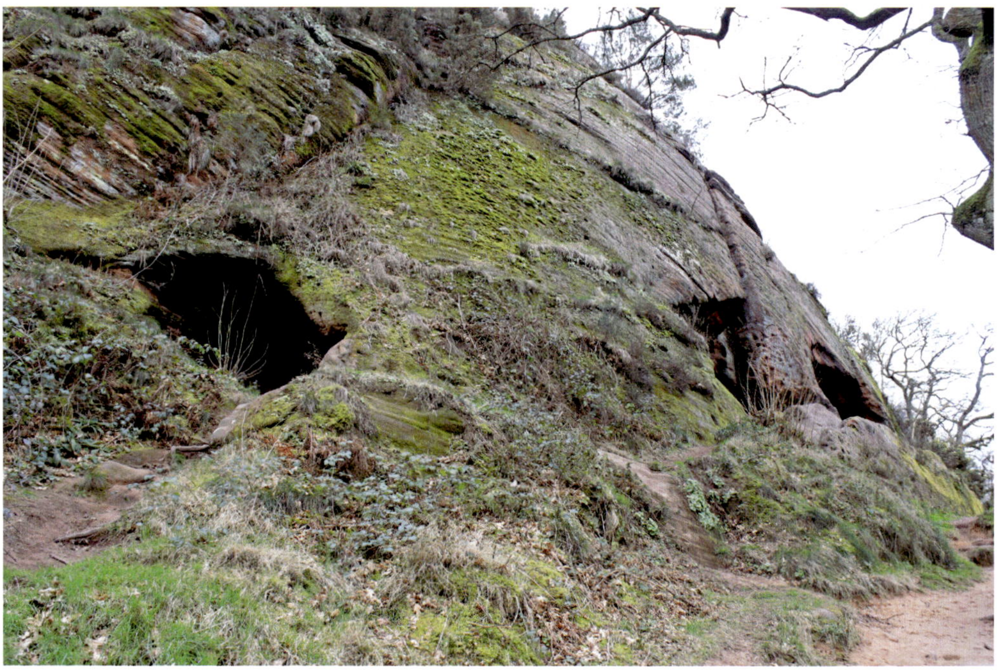

Nanny's Rock, Kinver.

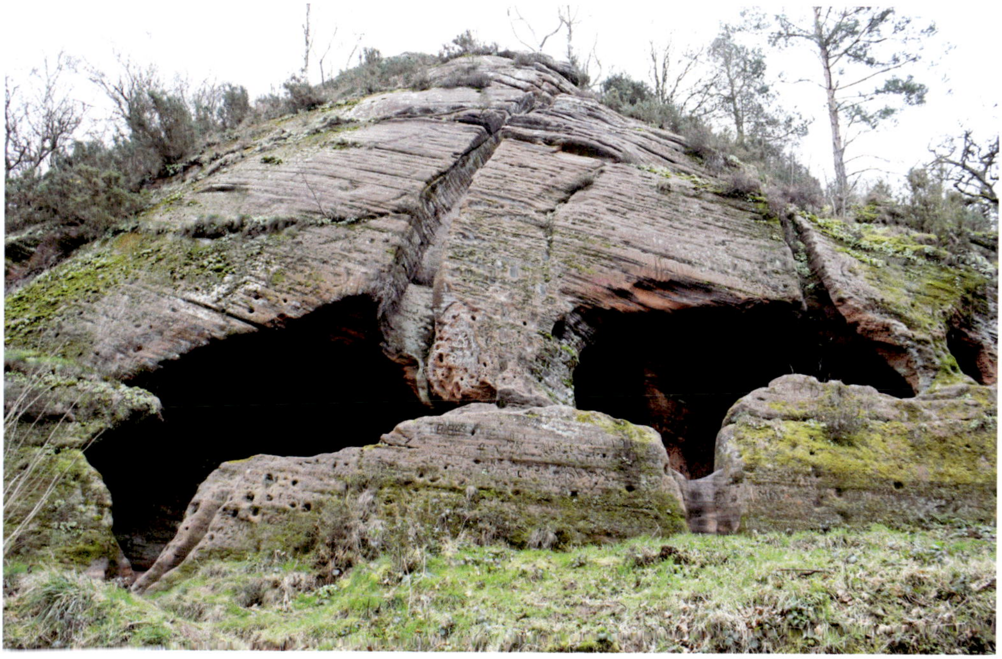

Nanny's Rock, with the Devil's Chimney visible in the centre of the outcrop.

Saxon period when Kinver's value was five times greater than that of Birmingham. The remains of a Bronze Age hill fort still mark the hilltop today, taking Kinver's history even further back in time. However, it is the houses carved into the cliffside by England's last troglodytes that make it truly extraordinary.

One of the earliest recorded mentions of the cave dwellings is from a 1777 journal by author Joseph Heely, who sought shelter from a storm with one of the families residing there. It's also believed that the unique rock houses, and the legend of two warring giants, inspired J. R. R. Tolkien when writing *The Hobbit*. In this tale, the rock houses of Kinver were occupied by a giant and his beautiful wife. Nearby, in Samson's Cave in Enville, lived another giant, a rival with a lustful eye for the Kinver giant's wife. One day, while the Kinver giant was collecting water, the Enville giant seized the opportunity to approach his neighbour's wife. He strode across the land to Holy Austin Rock, the home of his rival. Leaning through a window, he kissed the Kinver giant's unsuspecting wife. The Kinver giant, returning with the water, saw the kiss and, in his rage, hurled a great, long stone at the Enville giant, who was already racing back to his own cave. The rock narrowly missed the Enville giant but would stand firm in the ground as a lasting reminder against his return. Next time, the Kinver giant might not miss.

While in reality, it's unlikely that the caves were ever occupied by adversarial giants, they were certainly home to many generations of people. The final inhabitants of the cave dwellings at Kinver Edge vacated in the 1960s. The house, maintained as a museum, is now owned by the National Trust. But, some believe a spectral presence lingers. Locals and visitors frequently share tales of peculiar occurrences, unexplained footsteps, and faint voices echoing around the chambers. However, it is Nanny's Rock, an unrestored cave hidden deeper within the forest, that holds a more mysterious reputation. Window openings and a chimney have been carved into the soft sandstone, but it remains uncertain whether it ever functioned as a house. Many speculate that the caves served as a hideout for highwaymen or as secret storage for smugglers' loot.

Nanny's Rock is supposedly haunted by the ghost of a woman named Margaret, believed to have resided in the rock houses during the seventeenth century. As a local herbalist and healer, Margaret was renowned for her kindness and compassion. Yet, due to the fear that permeated the era, she was also suspected of being a witch. Consequently, she was driven away from civilisation to the caves, where she concocted healing potions for the daring few who sought her out. Numerous stories circulate about Margaret's ghost. The most common involves her appearance to those who are lost or in distress. Often described as a friendly spectre, she is said to offer guidance or solace to those in need before vanishing moments later. Little is known about her true identity, with the sole suggestion of her existence being a parish register that records the death of 'Margret of the Fox Earth' in June 1617.

Many years later, in the winter of 1850, a harsh cold descended upon the village of Kinver. Lottie, a young serving girl at the White Hart Inn, finished her long shift and walked home through the snowy streets. As she made her way through the alleys, she realised someone was following her. Fearful, she ran, but the heavy footsteps drew closer until she was struck on the head and fell unconscious. When Lottie awoke, she

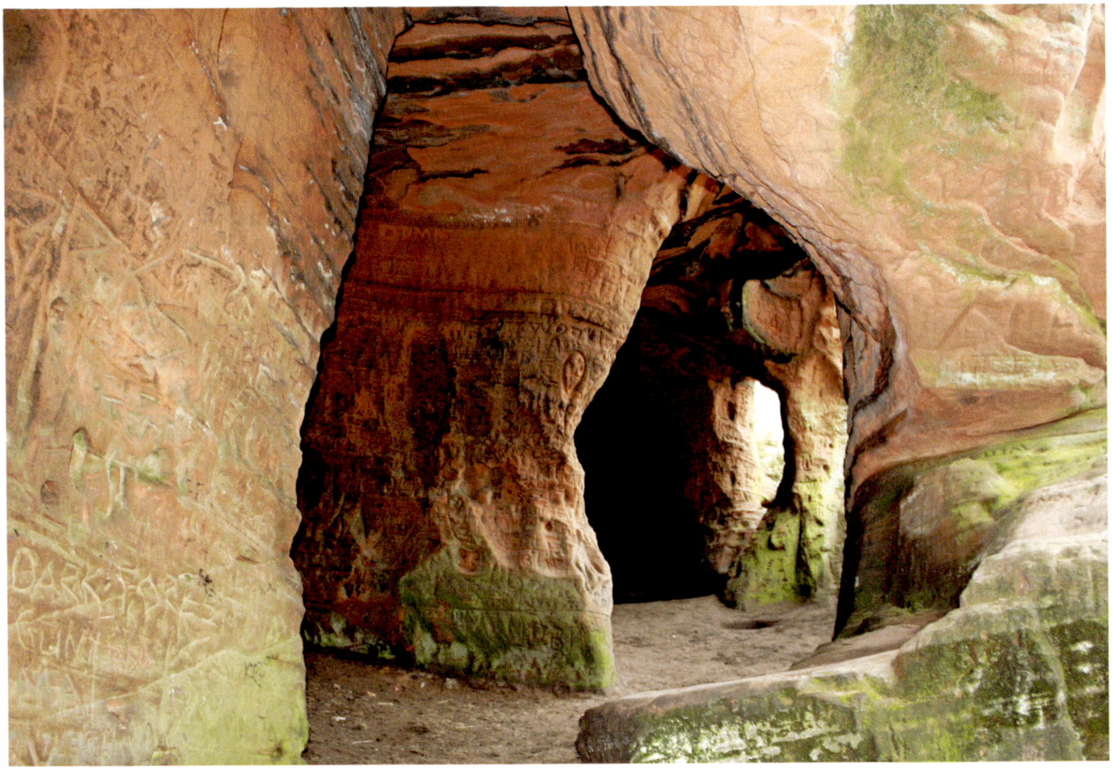

Inside Nanny's Rock, several rooms have been carved out of the cliffside, although none provide much living space.

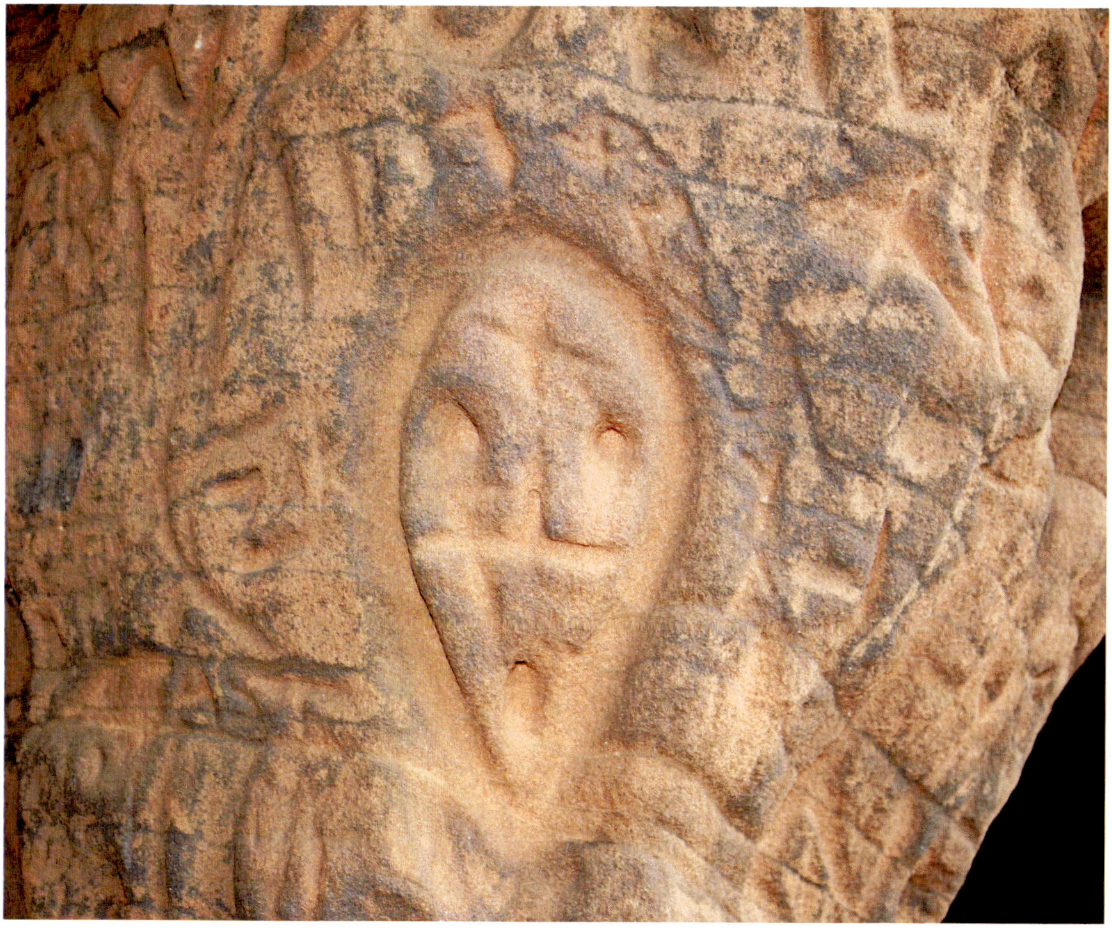

found herself slung over the shoulder of a large man. Stealthily, she used a pearl pin from her cloak to stab him, then escaped his grasp and ran through the woods across Kinver Edge. The assailant followed her tracks, but they mysteriously disappeared in a clearing, leaving only untouched snow. Panicked, the kidnapper fled into the night and fell over a cliff edge; his frozen body was later discovered by villagers. Lottie was never found, but visitors still claim to hear her soft humming on winter nights.

Lottie's kidnapper wasn't Kinver's only criminal in the nineteenth century. In December 1812, Benjamin Robins, a wealthy farmer, was returning to his home at Dunsley Hall when he was ambushed and shot at close range by William Howe. Known as a footpad – a highwayman who travelled on foot – William had targeted Robins specifically for his wealth. After firing the shot, William robbed the dying man and fled. Remarkably, Robins survived and was able to stagger back to Dunsley Hall. Unfortunately, he succumbed to his injuries ten days later. During that time, he identified his assailant, leading to swift justice. William Howe was sentenced to the gallows, and his body was ordered to be gibbeted in Kinver. This practice, a deterrent to would-be criminals, was underpinned by the belief that only those buried whole in consecrated ground would reach Heaven. The slow decay of a body in a metal cage

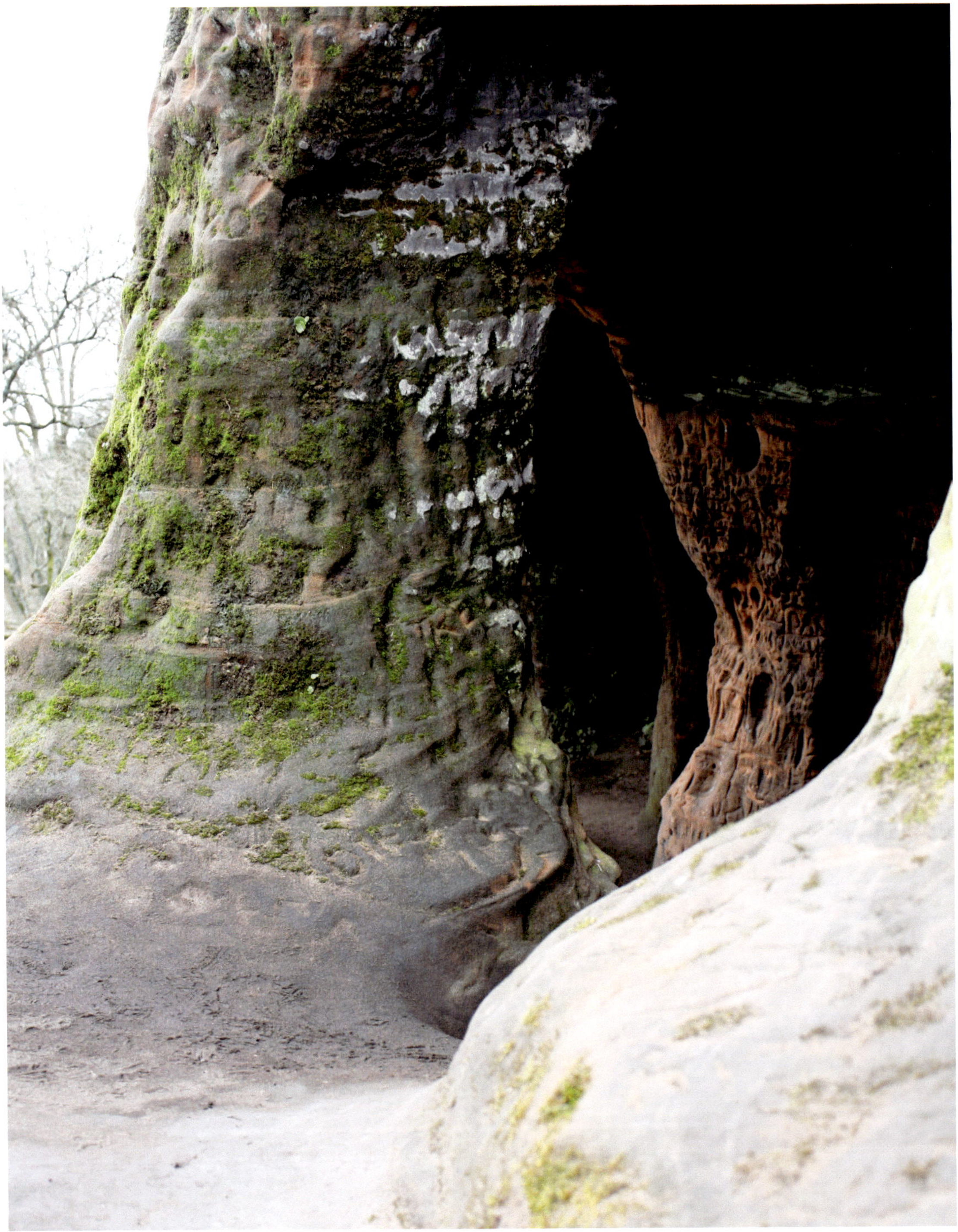

Whether Nanny's Rock ever had any occupants is a topic of debate, but its unique allure draws thousands of visitors to the Kinver Edge woodlands each year.

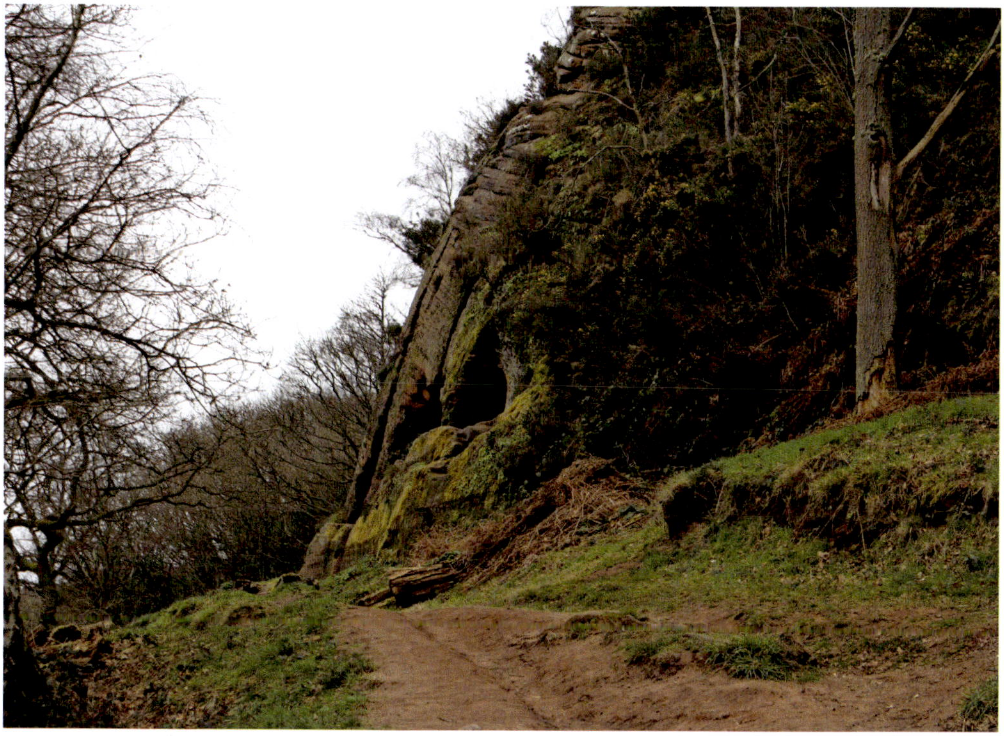

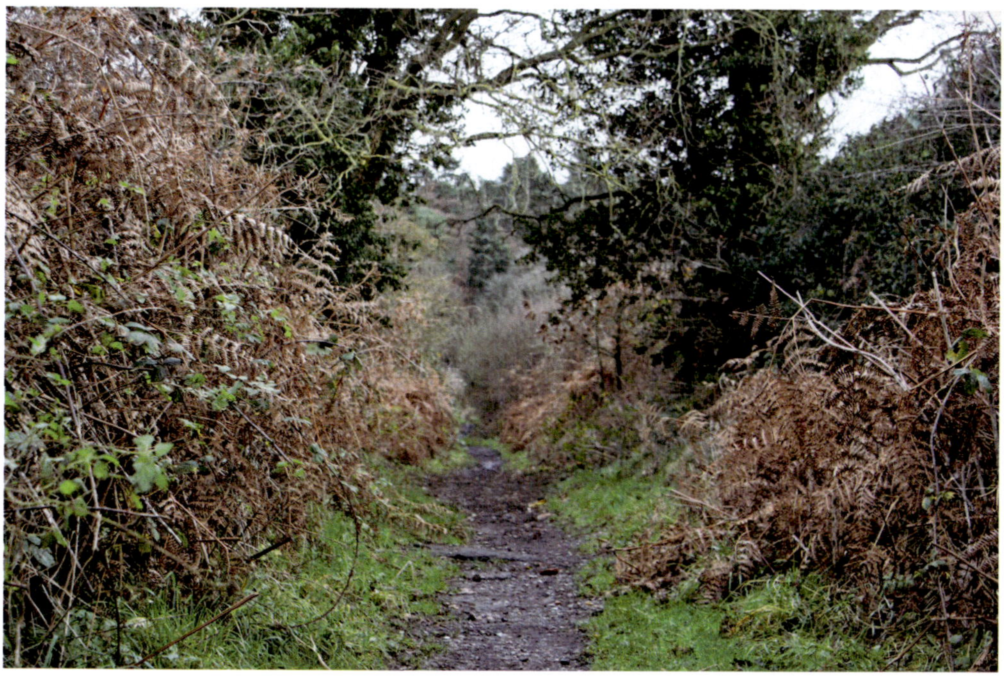

A few hundred yards away from Dunsley Hall, Gibbet Lane is a seldom-used narrow path reputed to be haunted by the ghost of William Howe.

was, to some, more terrifying than execution itself. Gibbet Wood and Gibbet Lane, named after this grim sentence, are said to be haunted by the restless and malevolent spirit of the infamous robber.

In 1872, a man walking through Whittington Common was startled by the sudden appearance of Howe's ghost. He lashed out with his stick, which passed right through the apparition. The ghost raised his arms and laughed menacingly as he faded away. In 1940, a local woman claimed to be followed down Gibbet Lane by a figure with a long neck that appeared broken. In 1957, another witness, Betty Howe, encountered a figure wearing a tricorne hat, brandishing a long-barrelled pistol in each hand. A similar encounter was reported by a policeman in 1972; he, too, saw a man in a tricorne hat, though this time without pistols. Whether through the legacy of gibbeting or simply the enduring spirit of a man addicted to banditry, William Howe continues to strike fear in death as he did in life.

Dunsley Hall, once the home of Howe's victim Benjamin Robins, is now a luxury hotel. It is believed to host several non-paying ghostly guests, though none of whom are thought to be the men from the previous tale. Some staff and visitors have reported a spectral figure appearing and then disappearing near the bar area. Additionally, there is an unknown gentleman who appears at a breakfast table in the mornings, vanishing when approached by staff who assume him to be one of their guests.

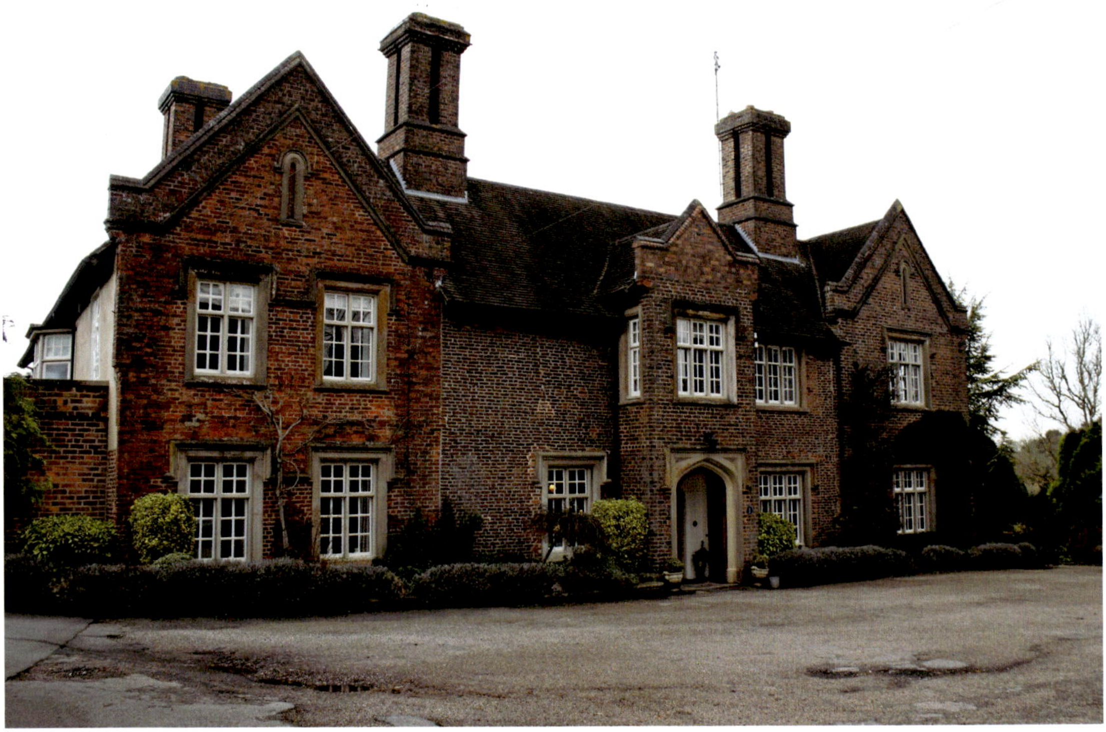

Dunsley Hall is now a popular hotel, where some believe a friendly ghost likes to join guests for breakfast.

Sandwell

To the east of Dudley is Sandwell, the second borough in our journey, which is named after a freshwater spring that bubbles up from the ground near Sandwell Priory. This 'sand well' was crucial for the monks of the nearby priory, providing them with clean water. The borough is home to several large towns, such as West Bromwich, Oldbury, Smethwick, and Wednesbury, but our visit to Sandwell begins in Cradley Heath, a place with its own set of tales and mysteries waiting to be explored.

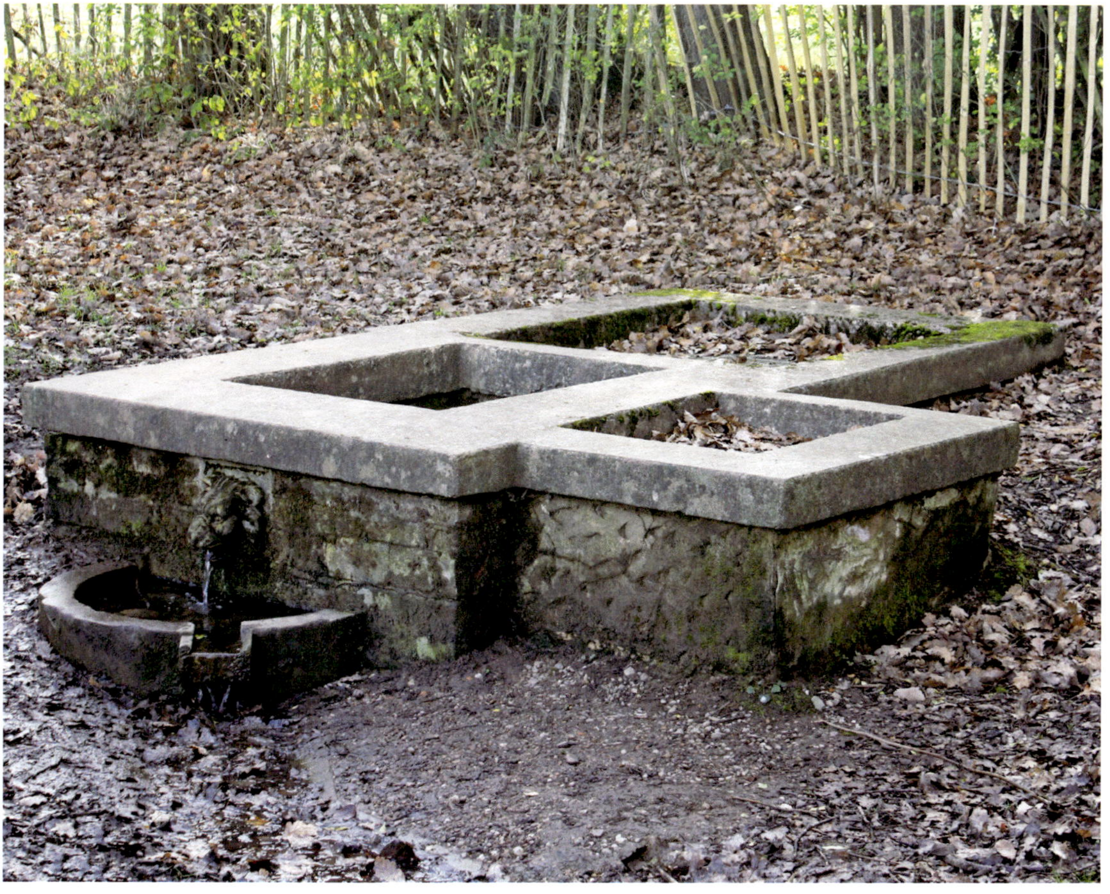

The wellspring where Sandwell gets its name still flows, albeit often a mere trickle.

Cradley Heath

Located in the southern half of the Black Country, the small town of Cradley Heath was founded upon the South Staffordshire coalfield that powered the region's nail and chain making industries. But while the collieries once scattered across the region are long gone, ghosts can still be found in some of the more contemporary buildings. In 1976, the peculiar happenings at Cradley Heath Ambulance Station were so unnerving that ambulance crews refused to stay there alone at night. The *Birmingham Evening Mail* reported accounts from the station's staff of eerie, disembodied footsteps echoing through the corridors after dark, and doors that opened unaided.

The following year, an unsettling presence at a house on Reddal Hill Road prompted a ghost hunt by officials from the local council. The tenant, Shirley McMahon, had merged the upstairs flat with a ground-floor second-hand shop into a single dwelling, and sought a reduction in rates due to the property's paranormal disturbances. Officials who went in to investigate the property were shown a bedroom and staircase where the ghost of an old woman was reputed to haunt. Mrs McMahon described hearing the ghost tapping the walls and crying several times, and that her husband and daughter both claim to have seen the spectre. 'I saw her in our bedroom one night,' her daughter said. 'Her face hidden in her hands as if she was crying.' Her husband, Ray, saw the same opaque figure on the staircase, but didn't tell his family until some time after the event. Despite their search, the officials left without any supernatural experiences, and subsequent years brought no further evidence of hauntings in the property. However, other buildings in Cradley Heath have a more pronounced and enduring history of ghostly occurrences, such as the enigmatic Haden Hill House.

Haden Hill House and Old Hall

The Haden Hill estate features two significant buildings: the older Haden Old Hall, dating back to the late 1600s, and the more recent Haden Hill House, built in 1878. George Alfred Haden-Best, who constructed the house, inherited the estate from a long line of Haden ancestors. The Hadens worked the land as farmers and grew their status over many generations, possibly starting as far back as the thirteenth century.

In medieval England, the land now known as Haden Hill was a hub of agricultural activity. Nearby Hayseech Mill was home to Elanor, a miller's daughter. Renowned for her blonde hair and bright blue eyes, Elanor captured the affections of one of the Haden family's sons. The young couple soon fell deeply in love, but the Hadens had plans for their son to become a monk at Halesowen Abbey, where he would be devoted solely to religious worship. Undeterred, the pair continued to meet in secret on the River Stour's banks, using a tunnel to and from the abbey for their secret meetings. However, when their relationship was exposed, they were forced to flee to avoid the wrath of the abbey's monks. With their cover blown, Elanor surrendered herself, knowing the punishment for the Haden boy would be severe if caught. Tragically, she was right. The monks trapped the young man in the tunnel and bricked up both ends as punishment for his indiscretion, sealing his fate. Elanor died a heartbroken woman. Since then, her distressed soul has been seen roaming the grounds, searching for her long-lost love. Numerous reports tell of her ghostly presence and the sound of wailing that seems to emanate from underground.

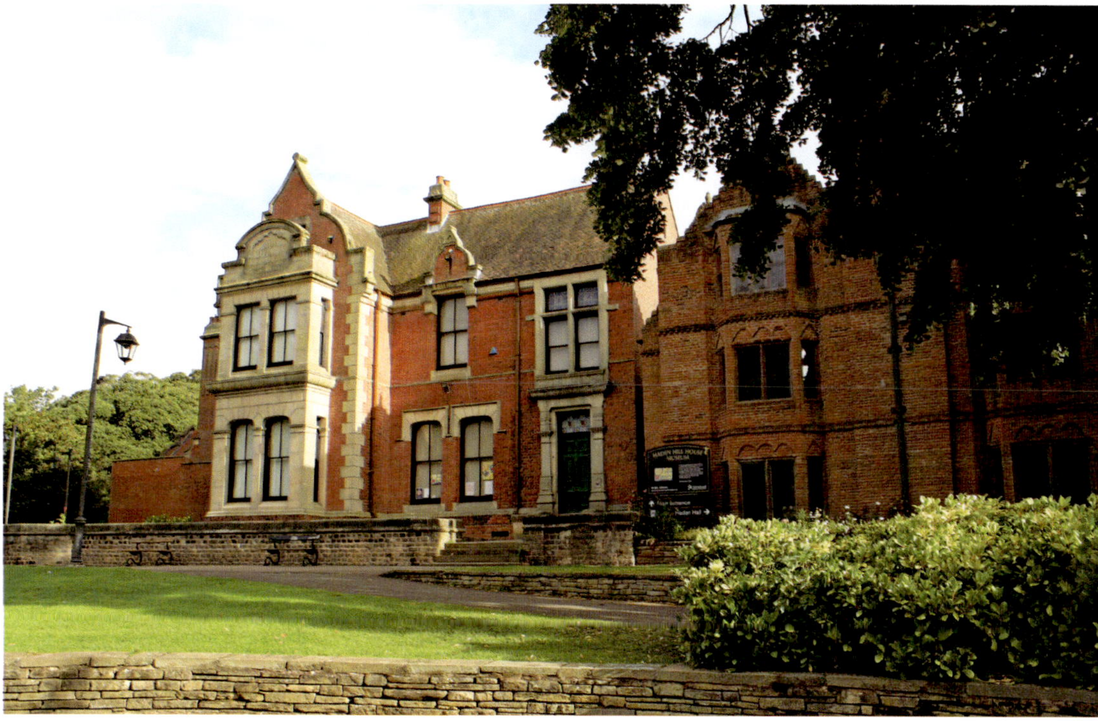

Haden Hill House and Haden Old Hall.

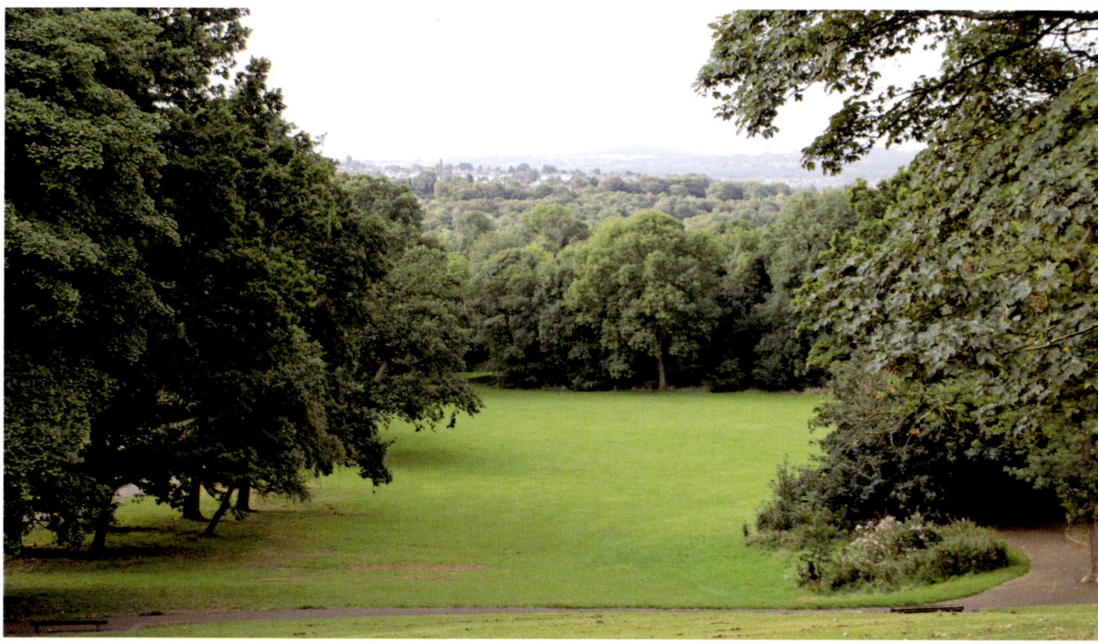

Both buildings offer a panoramic view overlooking 55 acres of parkland and stretching towards the scenic Worcestershire countryside.

While the story of Elanor and the monk might be just a popular local legend, it hasn't deterred investigators from seeking evidence of the couple and the elusive tunnel. In August 1950, the Rowley Regis Archaeological Society planned a ghost hunt in the cellars of Haden Hall. However, the event was delayed because an eighty-two-year-old woman, who claimed to know of another tunnel entrance possibly linked to the legend, was hospitalised. The *Birmingham Evening Despatch*, who published the story, reported that the only known tunnel entrances were bricked up a long time ago, but the hospitalised woman claimed to know of another entrance, possibly that of the legendary tunnel, somewhere nearby. The article also reported that several months earlier, a canteen worker at the hall reported hearing what she believed to be the ghost's presence in a room above her while working alone on the premises late one night. As to whether the old lady was ever released from hospital to join the search for the tunnel entrance is unknown, but another attempt was made in January 1974, when a group of scientists from Wolverhampton Polytechnic and Royal Hospital aimed to renew the search for the legendary spectres. Armed with tape recorders and the latest infra-red film and flash technology, they hoped to capture evidence during an overnight vigil. By then, the old hall had fallen into disrepair and was fenced off, but Warley Council granted the scientists special permission to enter, provided they signed waivers absolving the council of any responsibility. At midnight, during their investigation, they conducted an exorcism in the decaying mansion, led by three mediums who had joined them. One scientist described a medium entering a trance-like state in the kitchen, rumoured to be one of the most haunted parts of the building. The medium instructed the ghosts to depart, and afterwards, the team felt a change in the atmosphere, leading them to believe the ghosts had indeed left. However, this sense of accomplishment might have been premature, as just three years later, in March 1979, the *Birmingham Evening Mail* reported that ghosts still resided rent-free in the abandoned building.

Despite initial despair following a fire and a roof collapse, which seemed to doom any hopes of restoring the building, a group of enthusiastic apprentices partially rebuilt it in the 1990s. During their renovation work, they made an intriguing discovery in one of the top-floor rooms.

This legend traces back to the end of the Haden family's direct lineage with the birth of Anne Eliza Haden. Her father, then the sole heir to the family estate at age sixty-five, married Mary Kendrick, a nineteen-year-old cousin, to ensure the continuation of the Haden legacy and fortune. Mary gave birth to Anne Eliza, their only child. John, Anne Eliza's father, expressed his wish for his young wife to remarry after his death, stating in his will that the estate would pass to his daughter or, failing her marriage and producing an heir, to the children of Mary's second marriage. As years passed, Anne Eliza, a potential match for any wealthy suitor, became increasingly reclusive, eventually never venturing beyond the hall's grounds. She remained unmarried and childless until her death at age eighty-six. Some speculate she devoted her life to mourning her father, while others believe she aimed to protect the estate from the ravages of the Industrial Revolution by planting herself firmly in the hall's grounds. However, the conditions of her father's will led to suspicions that Anne Eliza was confined to the hall by her stepfather. Rumours suggested she was locked away in a top-floor room during suitors' visits to prevent any marriage and ensure his own children inherited the Haden fortune. For many years, even long after Anne Eliza's

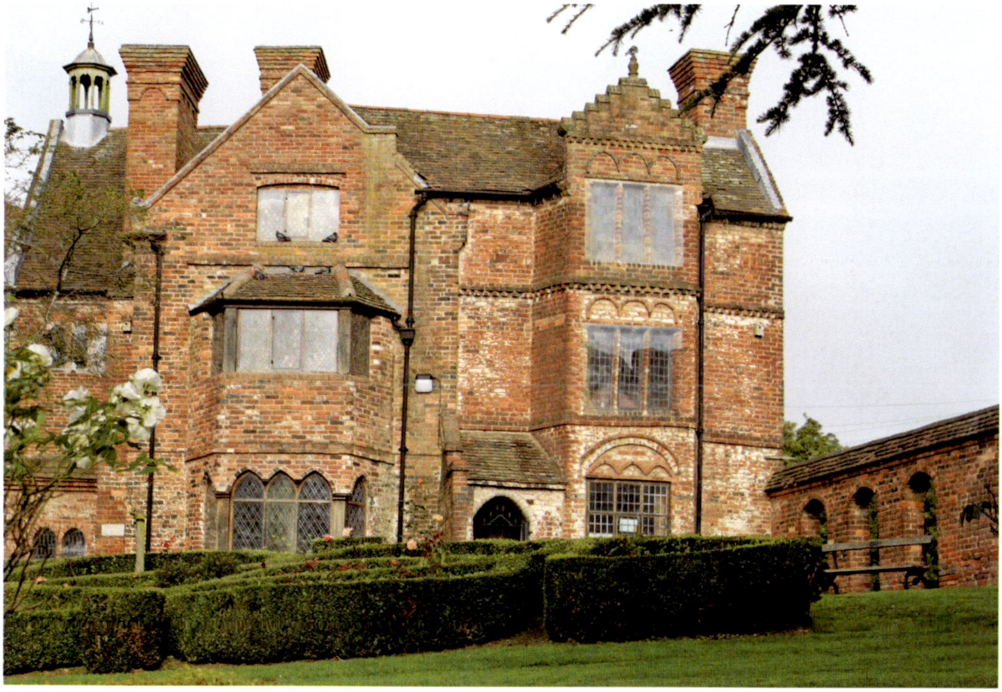

According to some stories, the face of a sad-looking woman has been seen staring out through the upper-floor windows of the Old Hall buildings.

death, visitors reported seeing a sorrowful face peering from a top-floor window, a room the apprentices later found to have barred windows.

Generations later, the estate passed to George Alfred Best, who adopted the Haden name as a condition of the inheritance, becoming George Alfred Haden-Best. Not wanting to live in the crumbling old hall, he ordered the construction of Haden Hill House and remains its only occupier. George, too, died without a direct heir but adopted two girls and lived as a philanthropist, founding local schools and educating over 800 students. Following his death in 1921, the estate was sold, and the title deeds were transferred to the Rowley Regis Urban District Council on 14 October 1922. After years of neglect and uncertainty about its future, the house was eventually transformed into a museum, now a popular destination for visitors and school groups.

Children who visit the house and hall have reported several mysterious occurrences centred around the servants' staircase. In one instance, a child excitedly told their parents about a lady wearing an old-fashioned costume dancing at the top of the staircase, although the parents looked up and saw no one. In another incident, a child adamantly refused to ascend the stairs, disturbed by the sight of an uninviting man with a stern expression, standing at the top. On a different occasion, a young child being carried upstairs suddenly began crying and screaming, pleading with their parents not to proceed further. The staff promptly directed them to an alternative staircase at the other end of the building. However, when they walked back across the building, near the top of the servants' stairs, the child's distress resumed.

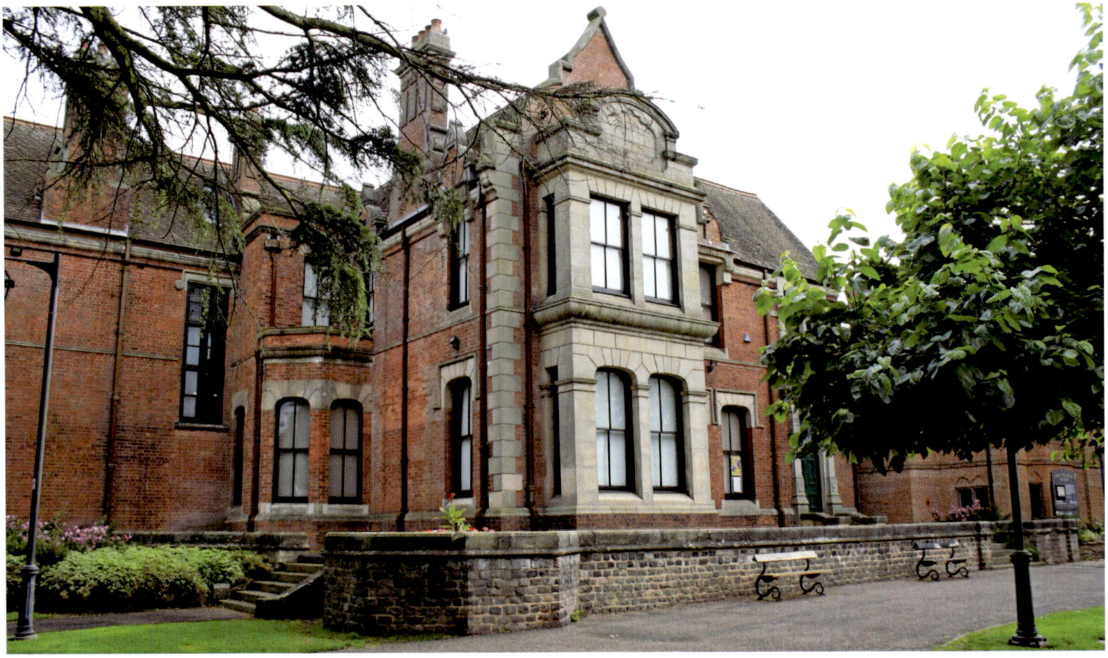

Haden Hill House.

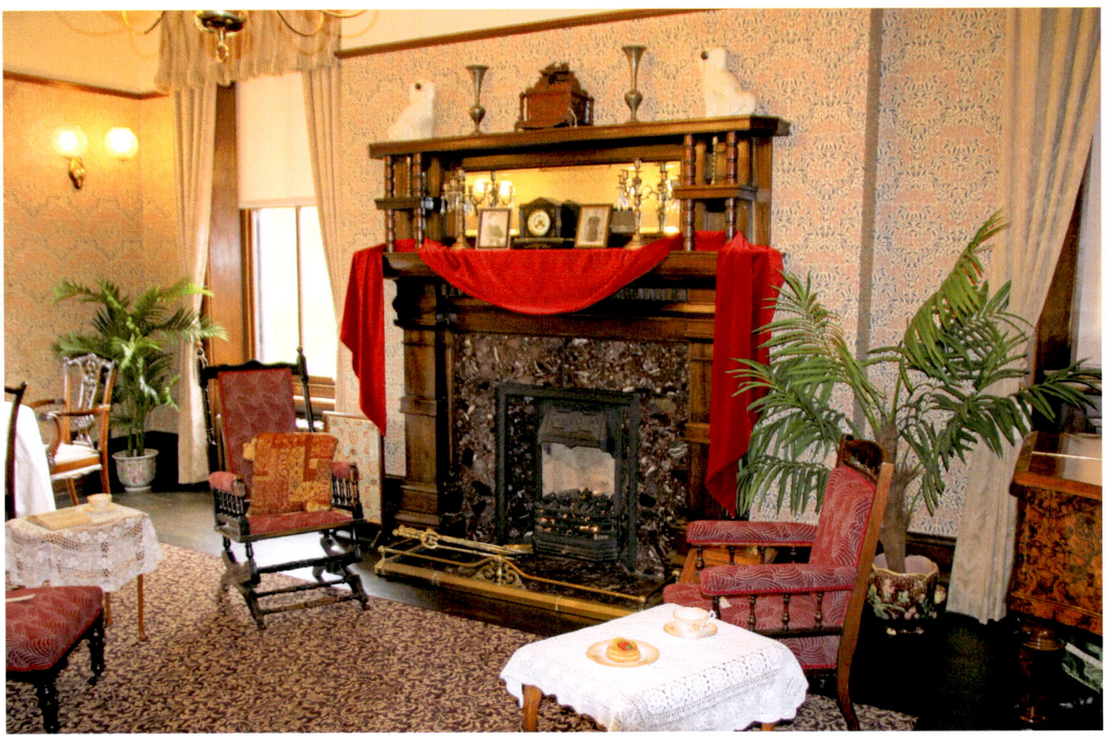

Inside Haden Hill House. (Courtesy of Terrence R. Alliband)

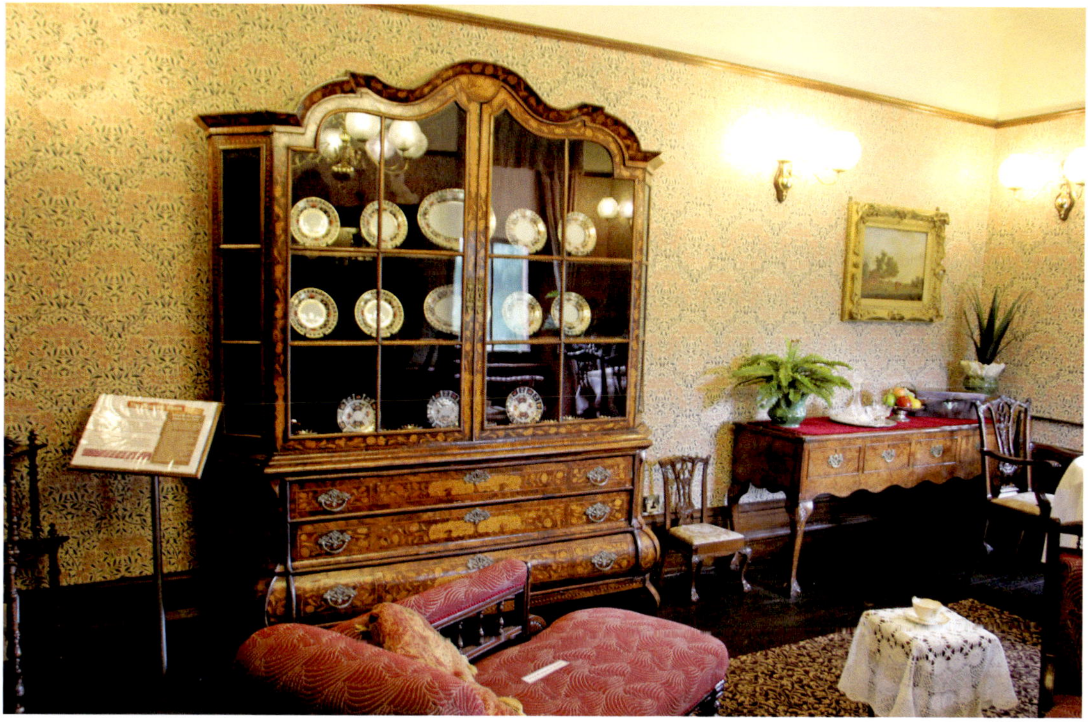

Inside Haden Hill House. (Courtesy of Terrence R. Alliband)

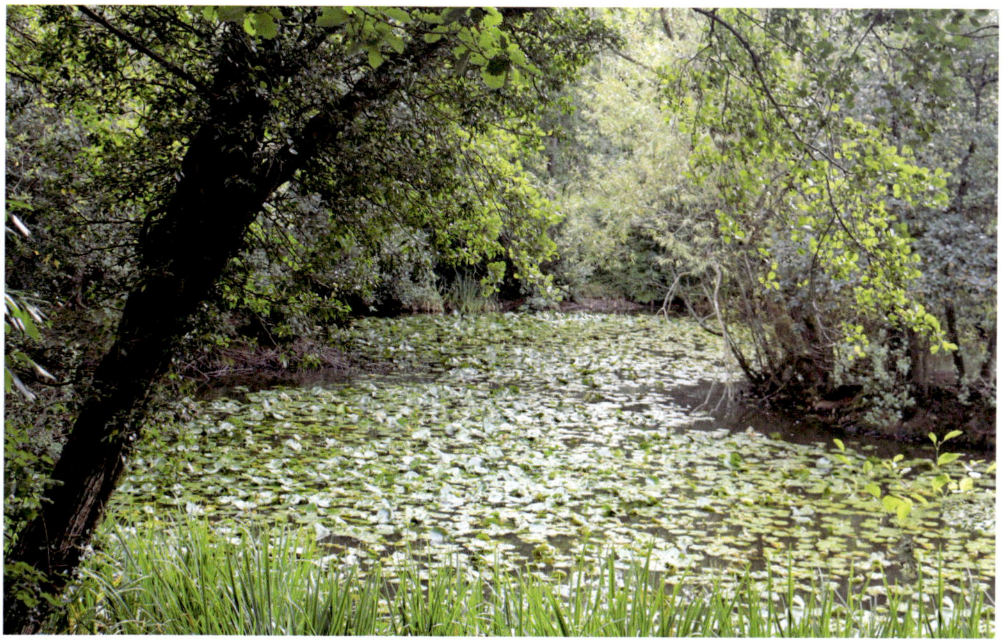

Away from the buildings, the pool in the parklands is also associated with sightings of a 'Blue Lady', spotted sitting at the water's edge.

Some areas of the Old Hall are off-limits to visitors. During one visit, several group members noticed a man disregarding a no-entry sign and entering a restricted area. They informed a staff member, who expressed gratitude and went to locate the man and guide him back to the public areas. However, after a thorough search, the staff member found no one in the restricted area.

Oldbury

Oldbury's history is deeply intertwined with the industrial boom, which provided essential employment for thousands of people. Following exhausting shifts in the mines and foundries, Oldbury's residents often sought respite in the town's numerous pubs. Among these was the Albion Inn on Tat Bank Road. In January 1981, the local press covered a story about a hunt for a treasure rumoured to be hidden within the pub. Previous licensees reported sightings of an old man's ghost, believed to be a former licensee who had concealed hundreds of pounds shortly before his demise. The new licensee, having never encountered the ghost, considered enlisting a spiritualist medium to communicate with the spirit in hopes of uncovering the hidden cash. However, by July of the same year, the Albion closed due to declining patronage.

Many other pubs in Oldbury also boast their own spectral stories, including the nearby Blue Ball Inn.

Blue Ball Inn

In June 1976, the Blue Ball Inn on Dudley Road East became the subject of eerie local gossip, with the Foster family, proprietors since the 1960s, at its heart. Glynis Foster, often found behind the bar, was the first to encounter the unexplained. One night, around 10.30 p.m., with the pub quieting down, she spotted an old man's pale face peering at her through a door's glass panel. Assuming it was a customer trying to get a last-minute drink, she went to tell him they were closing, only to find the space outside the door empty. Shrugging off the incident, Glynis went back to her duties, but was startled to see the same haunting face staring at her once again through the glass.

The phenomenon wasn't unique to Glynis, as regulars also reported seeing a 'strange white face' through the windows. Alice Foster, Glynis's mother, heard theories from patrons, including that it was one of the pub's old regulars. 'The pensioners who come in reckon it is the ghost of an old regular who died one night as he was walking home from the pub,' said Alice. Some say it's the ghost of William Parker, who was crushed to death by a falling chimney. Glynis, however, wondered if it was the ghost of a man murdered in the pub during Victorian times. When Alice finally saw the apparition for herself, she described it as an elderly man with a thin beard, wearing a tweed coat and muffler.

Whoever the ghost is, he has been spotted many times by several people, including a soldier who visited the pub while on leave. The soldier told Mrs Foster that he had walked past someone he assumed was the licensee in one of the pub's corridors. He was shocked to learn that no one else, including Mr Foster, was in the pub at the time. Upon hearing this, the young soldier turned white with fear. According to Alice, such a close encounter was rare, as the figure typically vanishes whenever anyone gets close to him.

Glynis said that despite the eerie feeling the sightings evoked, the family had become accustomed to seeing the old man around. However, this would soon change, as reported four years later in the same newspaper under the headline 'Pub with a spirit no one wants.' By then, the family had become troubled by unexplained sounds at night, lights swinging from the ceiling, and the pub's phone falling for no apparent reason. Mrs Foster admitted that while most occurrences could probably be explained, there was definitely 'an eerie atmosphere in some parts of the pub'. The worst affected was the daughter, Glynis, who saw the figure in her bedroom and had been frightened to stay there ever since. 'My room had a cold, hostile atmosphere,'

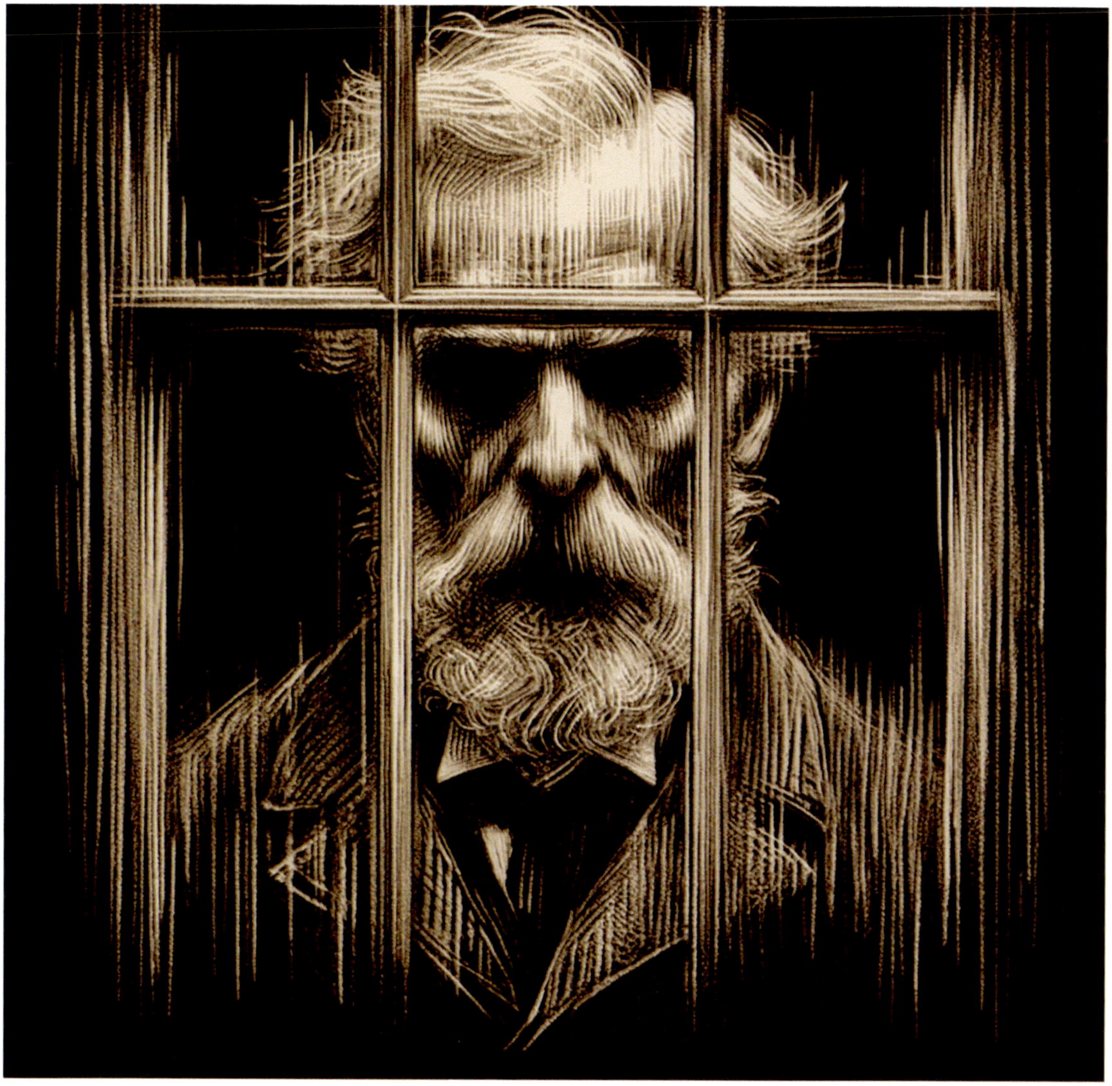

Many at the Blue Ball Inn saw the pale face of a former patron, longing for one final drink.

Glynis said, 'Yet no one has been hurt by the ghost.' At the time of her sighting, the family dog was also in the room and, according to Glynis, cowered in the corner, staring at a 'blue apparition'. After this incident, the dog refused to return to the room, and the frightened family felt they had no choice but to move out of the first floor of their home altogether.

A few years later, the Fosters left, and the once popular inn began to deteriorate. In April 1985, a development firm moved in to revamp the old pub before reopening it to the public. The focal point of this story for the local press was that the building's lonely ghost, now nicknamed Albert, would enjoy the company of the living. Sadly, this was to be the swansong for the Blue Ball Inn, which has since been demolished, taking the ghost of Albert with it.

Whiteheath Estate

The eighth floor of a high-rise flat is one of the last places you'd expect to encounter a ghost story, but for Dawn Green and her husband, Mike, living in the Whiteheath estate in Worley, paranormal activity became a part of daily life. As a newlywed couple seeking domestic bliss in a modern home, they were unprepared for the strange occurrences that began to unfold.

I met with Dawn, a distant relative of mine, at the Moat House in Tamworth, where she eagerly told me about when the strange occurrences started, shortly after moving into their flat in the late 1970s. It all started with small things, such as lights they switched off that turned themselves on again. Blaming faulty switches, Mike replaced several of them with new ones, but the lights continued to turn back on. All the clocks in the flat would sometimes stop at ten minutes to four. Again, no logical explanation for this could be found. 'I was the most sceptical person you could meet and just dismissed everything,' said Dawn. Initially, she didn't know what to make of the strange phenomenon and tried her best to ignore it. However, the oddities continued. On one occasion, Dawn set a saucepan on the hob, and left it simmering on the lowest setting before going about her usual kitchen tasks. When she turned back to the oven, she noticed that the dial had turned up to maximum on its own. 'I actually saw the knob move once,' Dawn added. For a while, she continued to dismiss these unusual experiences but eventually began to feel that they might not be alone in the flat.

Eventually, the unseen presence in Dawn's flat was nicknamed Josie. 'I kept saying, Josie, my bill's going to be sky high,' Dawn complained, as the dials on the oven began to move more frequently. 'But the worst thing,' she said, 'was when my TV started acting up.' It was a coin-operated television, common in the late 1970s, and managed by a rental company. Dawn called the company, who promised to send someone to fix it right away. Amazingly, the engineer arrived within just ten minutes. She opened the door to a man with straight, chin-length hair – more of a ladies' haircut – and a shirt buttoned right up to the top. Dawn thought it was an odd look, but then again, it was the 1970s. 'That was quick,' Dawn said as she invited the man in, but he offered no response. She led him to the front room, where the TV sat lifeless. Suddenly, she felt a wave of queasiness and a tingling sensation. Excusing herself, she left the silent man alone with the television and headed to a friend's apartment on the same floor, feeling

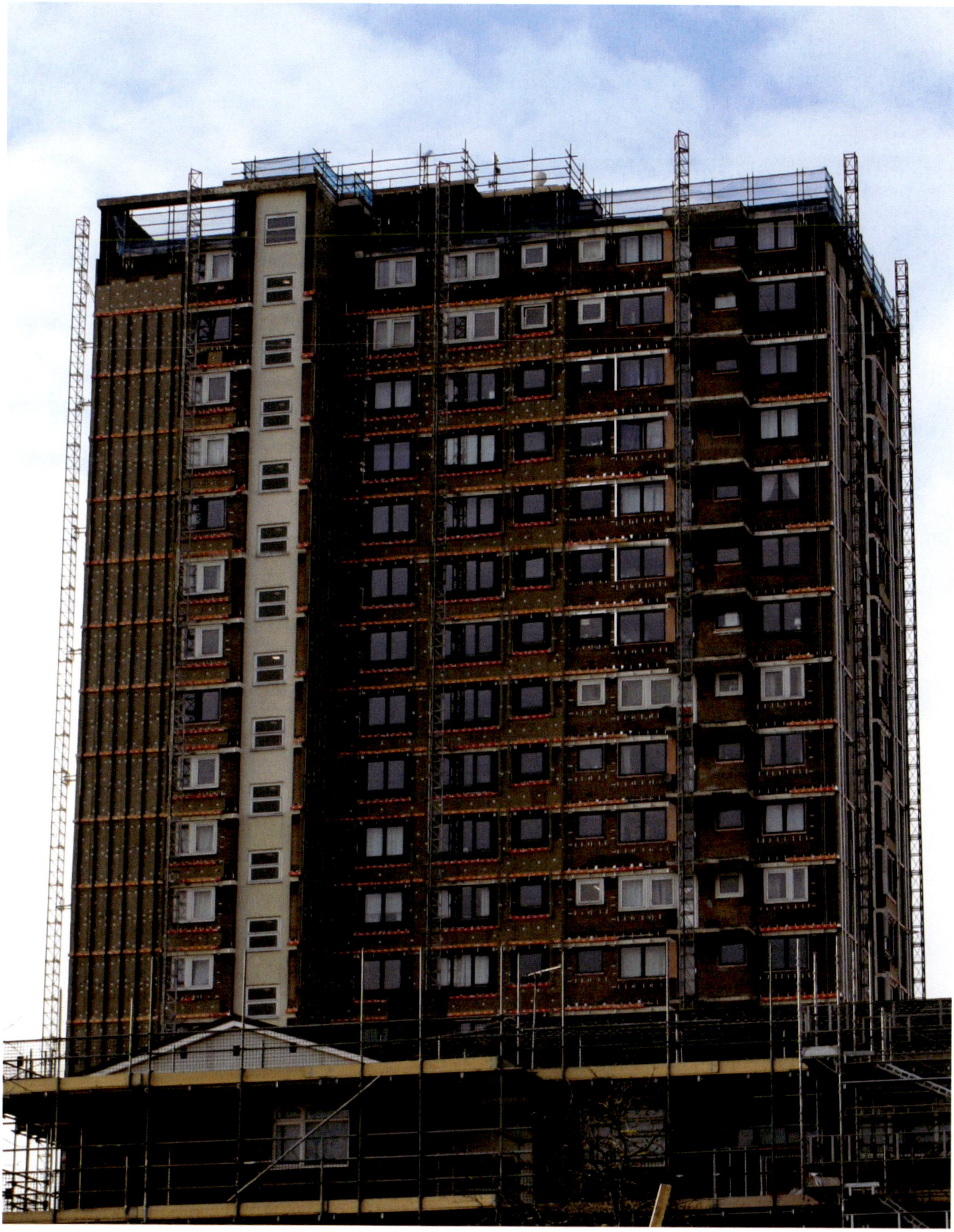

Most of the original flats on the Whiteheath Estate were demolished many years ago, with Darley House being one of the few that remain.

uneasy about the strange visitor. When she finally mustered the courage to return, she found the man holding the TV plug gently in his hands. He looked up at Dawn and said softly, 'Thank you,' before leaving. Around thirty minutes later, there was another knock at the door; it was the actual TV repairman. Puzzled, Dawn wondered, who was the man before, and whether he had something to do with Josie.

Dawn had reached her breaking point. 'Josie, stop this now, I don't like it,' she pleaded. 'If you are here, show yourself to me tonight and prove it!' At first, there was silence, and Dawn tried to calm down and go to bed. But then, unsettling events began to unfold. Doors started knocking, the letterbox flapped open and shut with a metallic clang, and the dog growled before cowering in a corner. 'Oh, I started to cry,' Dawn recalled. Realising they couldn't stay in the flat any longer, they hastily called a taxi. In a state of panic and confusion, Dawn, her husband, and the dog fled. 'How I got dressed, I'll never know,' said Dawn. She had grabbed the nearest thing to her, a leather jacket, and rushed down the stairs. Halfway down, she felt a tug on her coat, 'as if I was being pulled back'. The dog was on a step beside her, snapping at something unseen behind them. With no other choice, all Dawn could do was keep on running.

Eventually, Dawn and her husband reached the ground floor and ran out towards the road, where their taxi was due to pick them up. 'And that's when I saw her,' Dawn recalled. Standing before them was a fairly short woman, dressed entirely in white. She wore an old-fashioned hat adorned with white lace around the brim, and a white cloak draped over her shoulders. The mysterious figure looked at the bewildered couple and, with a blank expression, uttered, 'Please help me.'

At that moment, the taxi they had phoned a short while earlier approached from behind them. The driver came to an abrupt stop, his eyes fixed in stunned disbelief at the sight of the white-clad spectre. Without acknowledging the couple, the taxi driver quickly backed away, turned around, and sped off in the direction he had come from. When Dawn and her husband turned back to face the white woman, she quickly vanished into thin air. Dawn eventually reached her mother's house, a few miles away, and has never set foot inside that flat ever since.

Days later, a local paranormal investigation group decided to investigate Dawn's old home. After spending three nights there, they informed Dawn that it was one of the most paranormal active places they had ever encountered. They even agreed to share their findings with the local press, with their findings featured in the *Black Country Bugle*. When I asked whether she believed in ghosts, Dawn said, 'I have to believe, because of what's happened to me. What I've seen, actually seeing it with my own eyes, and the experience of it all.'

Having met Dawn to hear her story, one remarkable aspect is her reluctance towards these experiences. As a person who is usually sceptical, I can attest that many would dismiss such tales as figments of imagination or attention-seeking. However, Dawn insists she doesn't invite these occurrences and avoids actively seeking them out. Despite this, people who read her story in the newspaper sought her out, inviting her to join paranormal investigation groups or requesting her to undergo spiritualist readings. Each time, she refused.

Who Josie was, exactly, remains a mystery. The block of flats that hundreds of people once called home no longer exists, and with its demise, so too went the spirits who haunted it.

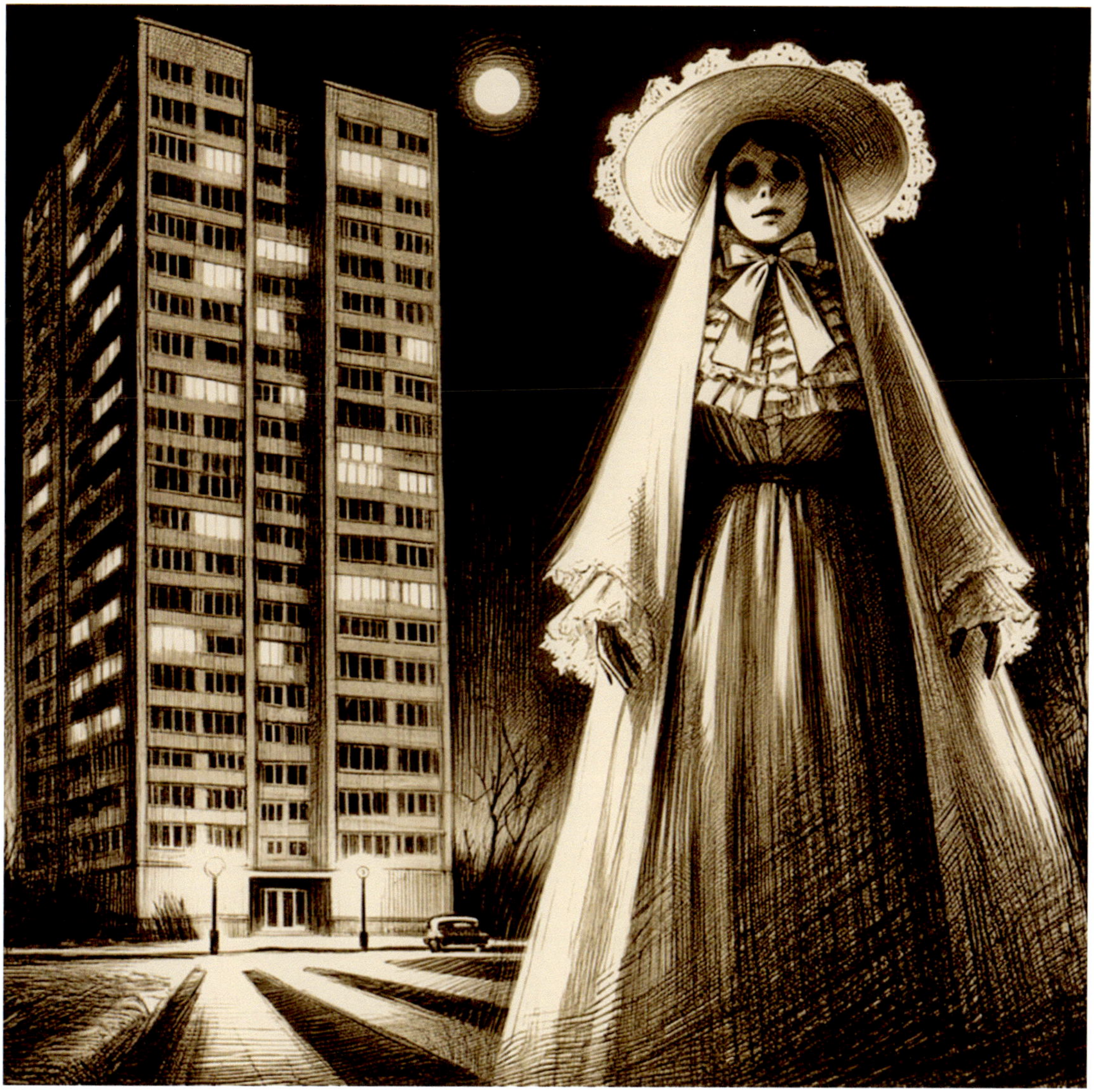

The sighting of Josie by several witnesses outside their low-rise flat was the climax following a gradual build-up of unexplainable events.

Warley Woods

Sandwiched between the eastern edges of the Black Country and the city of Birmingham, Warley Woods is a beautiful parkland where people from the surrounding towns like to walk and relax. The history of Warley Woods dates back to the Norman Conquest, where early settlers and monks from Halesowen Abbey farmed the land. This era of devoted care ended with the Dissolution of the Monasteries, and the land fell into private hands. In the late 1700s, the land was transformed into a country park for a manor house, and though the house no longer stands, the park retains its beauty, even preserving faint trough and furrow marks from its agricultural past.

With a history spanning a millennium, Warley Woods is rife with supernatural tales, the most famous being that of the Grey Lady. Her story begins in 1822, when Samuel Whitehouse was found dead with severe head injuries near a road where an old water tower now stands. The events leading to his tragic end were unknown, but his stolen watch and money led many to suspect murder. The prime suspect became his brother-in-law, Joseph Downing. Earlier that day, the two men were shooting wildfowl and, afterwards, parted ways for their homes. However, Downing returned to search for Sam after his horse was discovered riderless and in a state of extreme terror. Downing was the one who found Samuel's lifeless body but was later arrested and charged with his murder. At trial, Downing's defence suggested that a well-known local ghost, the 'Grey Lady', had startled the horse, causing a fatal accident. With no concrete evidence against Downing and numerous accounts of the Grey Lady's sightings, he was acquitted.

In the late nineteenth century, Sir Hugh Gilzean Reid, Member of Parliament and the new owner of Warley Abbey, was renowned for hosting lavish gatherings. These parties attracted notable artists and writers, one of whom was Harry Furniss, a distinguished illustrator for leading news publications. There are several versions of his tale, but according to one account published in 1936, Harry's encounter occurred at the end of one such party. It was around midnight; the guests' brandy glasses were empty, and their cigars were reduced to stubs. The household was winding down, with

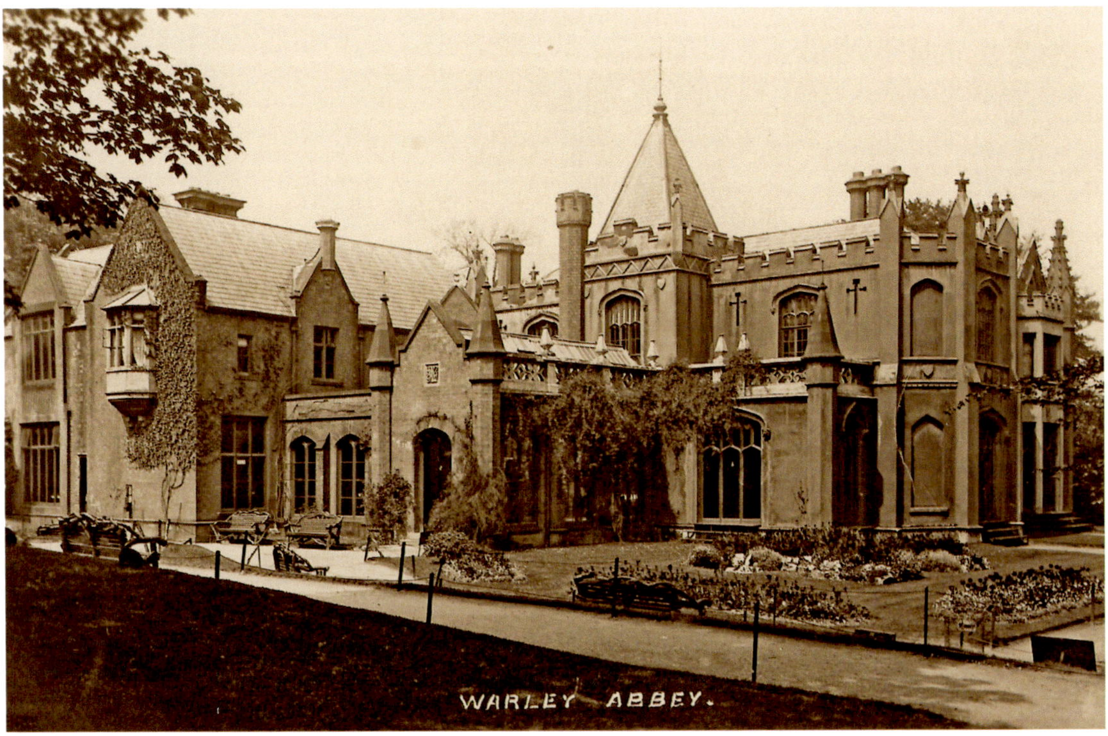

Warley Abbey was demolished in 1957 and is remembered in old photographs and postcards.

most preparing to retire for the night. Harry, however, lingered alone in the smoking room, savouring his last cigar in solitude. It was then that the room's atmosphere shifted dramatically. Without a sound, the door to the smoking room swung open. A shrouded grey figure, with arms uplifted and head bowed, entered the room. This ghostly apparition glided across the floor, passing right in front of a stunned Harry before vanishing into thin air. The sighting left an image so vivid in his mind that Furniss immediately sketched what he saw. His depiction was later published in the esteemed satirical magazine *Punch* – although much searching for a copy of this has yielded no results.

The Grey Lady's identity is shrouded in mystery. Some believe she is Lucy Galton, murdered without justice, while others suggest she's a heartbroken Galton heiress who took her life on the abbey grounds. The tragic narratives surrounding the Galton family make them likely candidates for the apparition. Warley Woods' hauntings aren't limited to the Grey Lady. Another ghost, a Chinese man in traditional attire, has also been sighted. Contrasting stories surround him: one depicts him as a jealous servant who murdered Lucy Galton, while another portrays him as a grateful man who found solace with a kind-hearted old lady.

The stories of Warley Woods continue to captivate and mystify. With its deep historical roots, the woods have seemingly become a sanctuary for restless spirits. Walk along its paths today, and you might just catch a glimpse of its illustrious past.

Delville Road

The following story was shared with me by Marie Collins, which took place in the early 1980s. At the tender age of five, Marie and her parents settled into their new, three-bedroom house on Delville Road. This home, a source of countless happy memories, also harboured a mystery that would unsettle the family and remain vivid in Marie's memory decades later.

As a young girl, Marie often played 'families' in the hallway with her small assortment of dolls. Since her collection was limited, she creatively used makeup bottles as extra members of her pretend family. She often played in the hallway, on a cosy burgundy carpet that was far more comfortable than the cold floor of the kitchen where her mother, Margaret, could usually be found busily working away. With a small doll in one hand and a bottle of face cream borrowed from Margaret's makeup bag in the other, Marie looked upwards and saw a strange figure standing at the top of the stairs. Unlike the typical apparitions often reported – monks, grey ladies, or Victorian-clad phantoms – the person in young Marie's presence was distinctly a soldier dressed from top to bottom in green army camouflage. Marie said he was only a young man of medium height and brown hair. He never moved or tried to interact with Marie in any way. Instead, he remained still, his eyes fixed on Marie, his arms hanging motionless by his sides. Although not frightened by the soldier, Marie ran to the kitchen to tell her mother. 'Mom, mom,' she exclaimed. 'Who's that boy at the top of the stairs?' She grabbed her baffled mother's hand and led her to the hallway, but when they looked up the stairs, the young soldier who had stood there so vividly only a few minutes earlier was gone.

Strange things soon began happening in other parts of the house and to other family members. One night, Marie's nan came to stay with the family and slept in the spare room. 'We all kept our bedroom doors slightly ajar at night,' said Marie, who lay awake in her bed. Through the gap in her door, she could see the glow of light at the top of the landing, which went on, off, on, off, rhythmically like someone flicking the light switch. The following morning, Marie overheard her nan talking to her mother, describing the same thing happening last night, and was determined that no one was there. Her nan finished by insisting that this was the last time she would stay the night in their house.

Marie's mother, Margaret, still knew the old couple who lived in their house before them. One day, she decided to visit them in their new home, a bungalow in town. She brought with her an old photograph of a boy the family found while digging

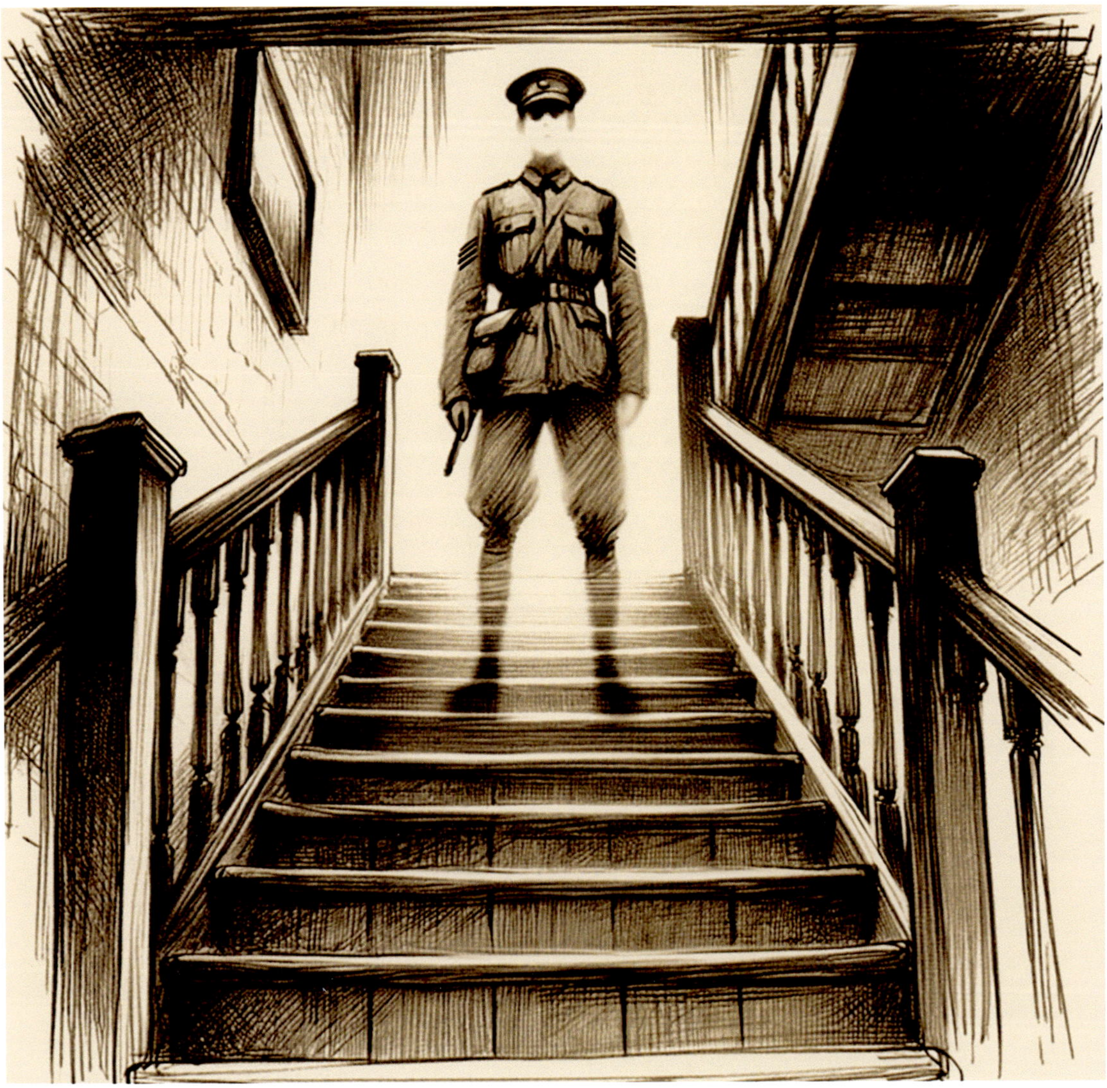

Children tend to witness ghosts more often than adults. Perhaps there's more truth in their imaginary friends than we know.

in the garden, hoping to find out who he was. The old lady looked solemnly at the picture and then revealed to Margaret that the boy was her son. Rising from her chair, she fetched another photograph, this one showing her son, by now a young man, as a soldier dressed in green camouflage. With a heavy heart, she shared that he had tragically passed away many years earlier in what was now Margaret's house, succumbing to a gangrene-infected shrapnel wound.

When Margaret got home, she decided to call a vicar. Partly to end the strange experiences in the home, but also from a sympathetic perspective, feeling that the soldier's spirit should be able to move on. 'I can still remember the smell now,' said Marie, who recalled a vicar's visit a few days later. She watched in fascination as the man walked throughout their home, reading from a bible and sprinkling holy water, while a young assistant followed behind, waving a smoking ball filled with hot coals and incense. Ever since that day, the strange things were no more. 'I'd like to believe,' Marie said, 'that the young soldier found his peace as well.'

Haunted Houses of West Bromwich

I generally avoid reporting on hauntings in private dwellings, mostly out of consideration for the current residents. However, while delving into several decades of regional newspapers, I noticed a concentration of haunted homes in the West Bromwich area.

Reports of supernatural occurrences around Newton Road began as early as 1965. But it was a short distance away, on Lincoln Road, where things became particularly intriguing in the early 1980s. The hauntings in question took place in a post-war council estate, home to the Grainger family. Barry, then aged seventeen, refused to sleep in his bedroom after encountering a ghost. 'I just cannot sleep up there,' Barry stated. 'I saw the figure, and it lingered for five or ten minutes.' Barry's experience left him so fraught with anxiety that his mother consulted a doctor, but no medical issue was found. 'We've all been under strain because of these events,' remarked Sheila, Barry's mother. 'Barry is hardly ever here now and refuses to go upstairs alone.' The family describes the ghost as an elderly man with snowy hair, often seen kneeling and praying at night. Mrs Grainger noted that the ghost sometimes cries out or walks up and down the stairs. At the time, the Graingers had not considered seeking an exorcism. Interestingly, the local MP, Mr Peter Snape, planned to visit the estate to investigate the matter himself.

A year later, the hauntings in a property on Nelson Street intensified to the point that they drove the family out of their home. The house was occupied by Mrs Monica Brown, whose sister, Pauline, had tragically died in the living room just a year prior to the story hitting the news. Since then, Monica and her young family experienced numerous supernatural occurrences. Monica recounted waking up two days after her sister's death, hearing a voice calling from the room where Pauline had passed away. 'I know I'm not imagining it,' Mrs Brown insisted, 'because Ian heard it too.' Ian, her thirteen-year-old son, had also heard the voices emanating from that room, and his twelve-year-old sister claimed she saw the ghostly figure of a woman in a red dress standing in her bedroom. In response to these unsettling events, a local priest was called to offer prayers with the family, stopping short of performing a full exorcism.

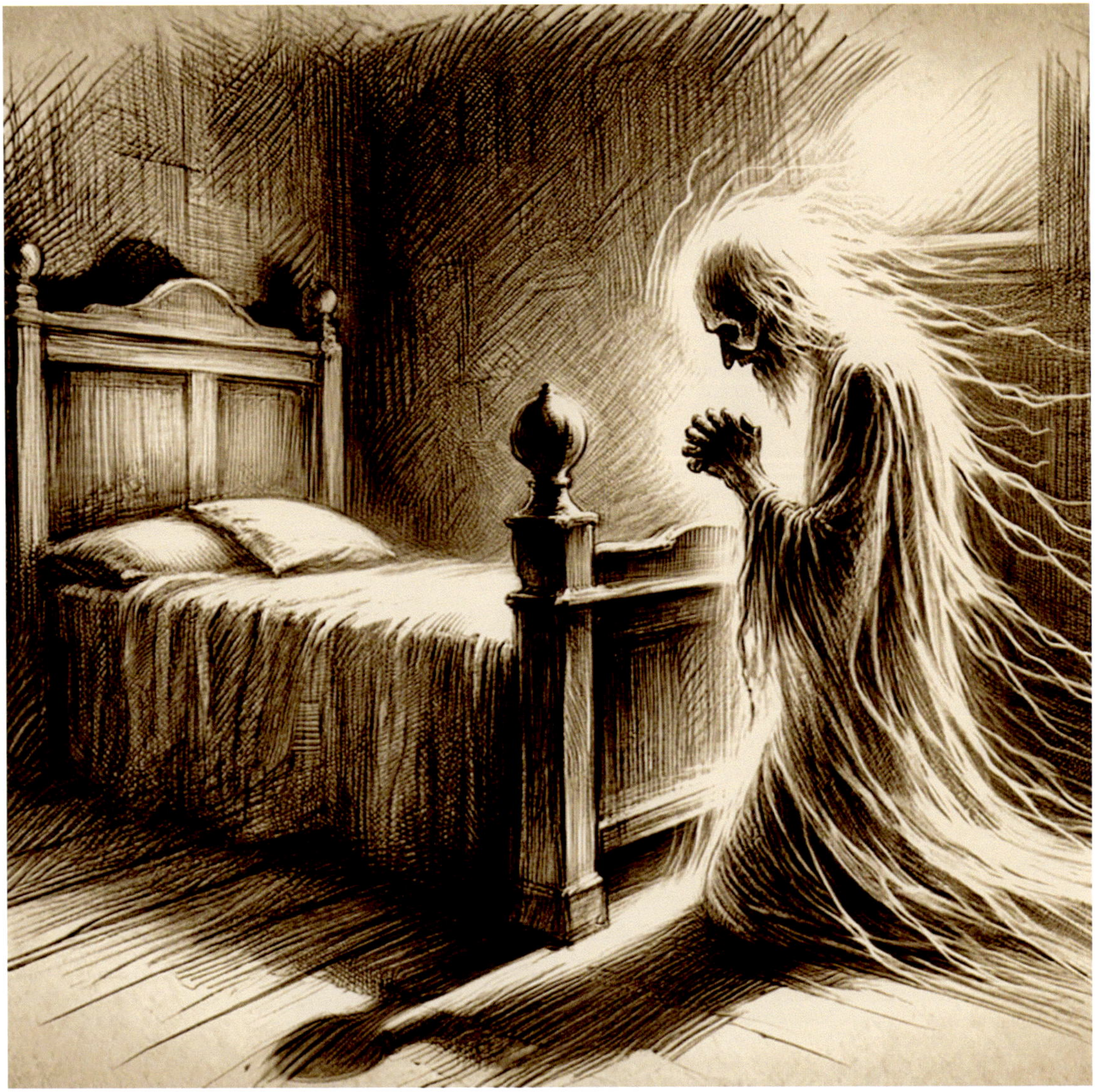

It's hard not to sympathise with young Barry and his family, who shared their home with the ghost of a kneeling elderly man.

However, the mysterious voices continued unabated. After enduring several months of this ordeal, the council finally granted Monica's request to be rehomed, though they attributed the move to social reasons rather than acknowledging the supernatural aspect.

A couple of decades later, in 1998, another family found themselves compelled to leave their home, this time on Florence Road. Miss Wendy Evans lived in the two-bedroom house with her boyfriend, Mr Smith, and their three-year-old son. They began experiencing strange occurrences around eighteen months after moving in. 'We both saw wispy, white apparitions of a man and a woman on the stairs, appearing separately or together at different times over a few weeks,' Miss Evans

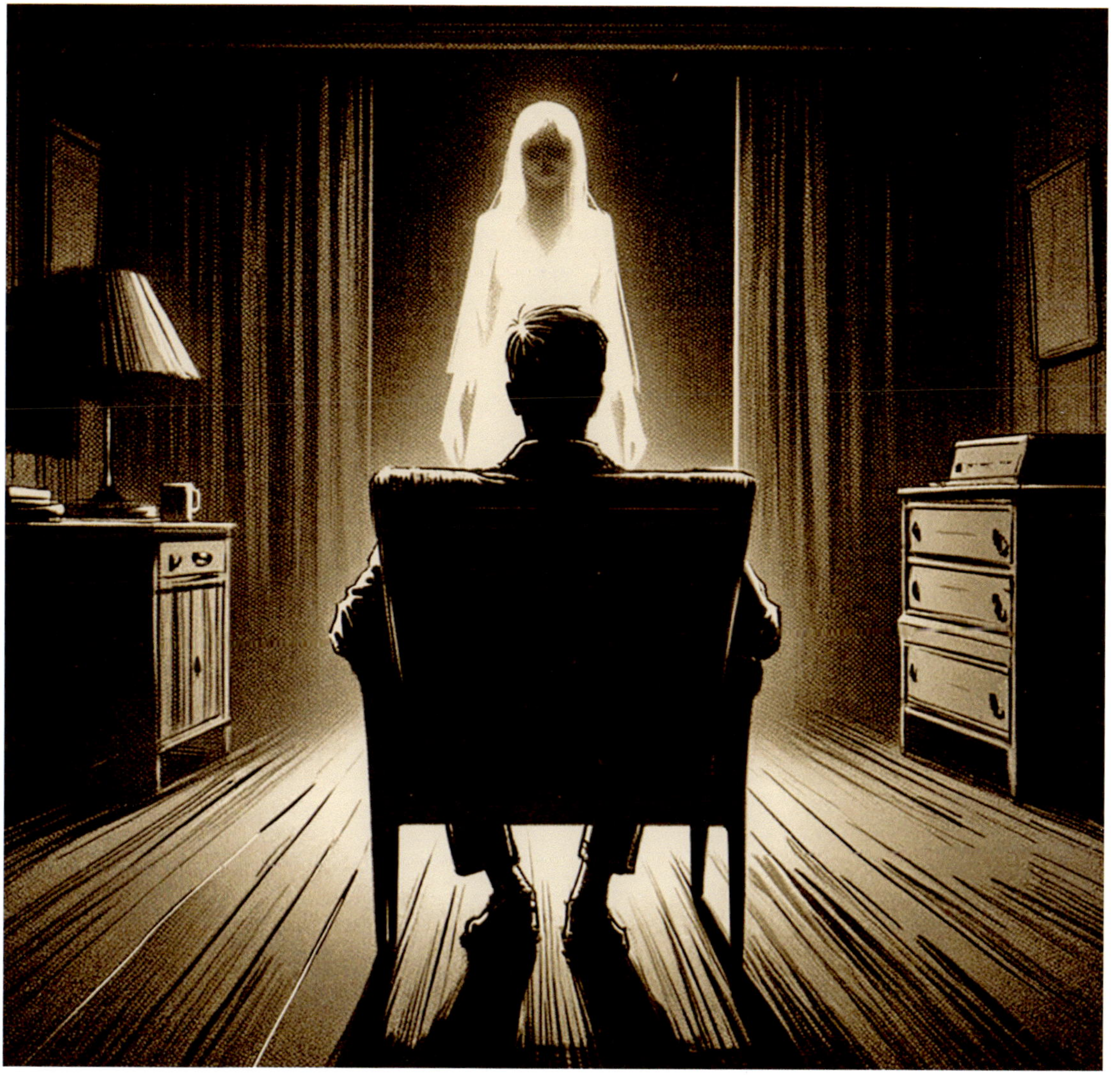

An artist's impression of the Ghost of Florence Road.

explained. These spectres were accompanied by the scent of sickly perfume. 'We called in a Methodist minister to perform an exorcism,' Mr Smith recounted, 'but it seemed to worsen the situation instead of improving it.' The couple also sought assistance from a local paranormal investigator, but their efforts were unsuccessful in calming the restless spirits. The final straw came one Friday night while the family was in the lounge watching television. The apparition of the woman materialised in the doorway, fixing Barry with a piercing stare and outstretching her right arm.

Curious about the house's history, the couple discovered it was built in 1896 and identified the name of its first occupant, but they found no clues explaining the persistent hauntings. Ultimately, the family decided to move in with Wendy's sister until they could find alternative accommodation.

Bromwich Hall – the Manor House

Surrounded by terraced housing that winds around its perimeter, Bromwich Hall's striking black-and-white timber frame marks a vivid contrast to its modern surroundings. Constructed around 1270, the building is a remarkable survivor from the region's medieval past. Built by Richard de Marnham, a wealthy merchant who sought to improve his social standing through marriage into nobility, the hall was the lord of the manor's residence. It featured a chapel and farmhouses, integral to the life and disputes of the local community. The heart of this historic complex is the medieval great hall, a vast open area once bustling with feasts, gatherings, and the resolution of disputes between local farmers and settlers. The buildings that encircle the great hall, like the ornately carved gatehouse, were added in subsequent centuries. A closer inspection of these structures reveals apotropaic marks, V-shaped carvings believed to ward off evil spirits and witches' spells. These marks, etched into the beams, seem to have served their purpose well, as none of the spirits residing at Bromwich Hall are deemed malevolent or frightening.

One such ghost is that of a monk, who peacefully roams the grounds near the hall and its moat. His silent, solemn presence has led locals and visitors to affectionately name him Henry, although his connection to the building remains a mystery. Maybe he is the same monk spotted crossing the M5 motorway near Sandwell Priory, less than 3 miles away, but that remains pure speculation. Over the centuries that followed, the estate changed hands among various nobles until the 1880s, when the buildings

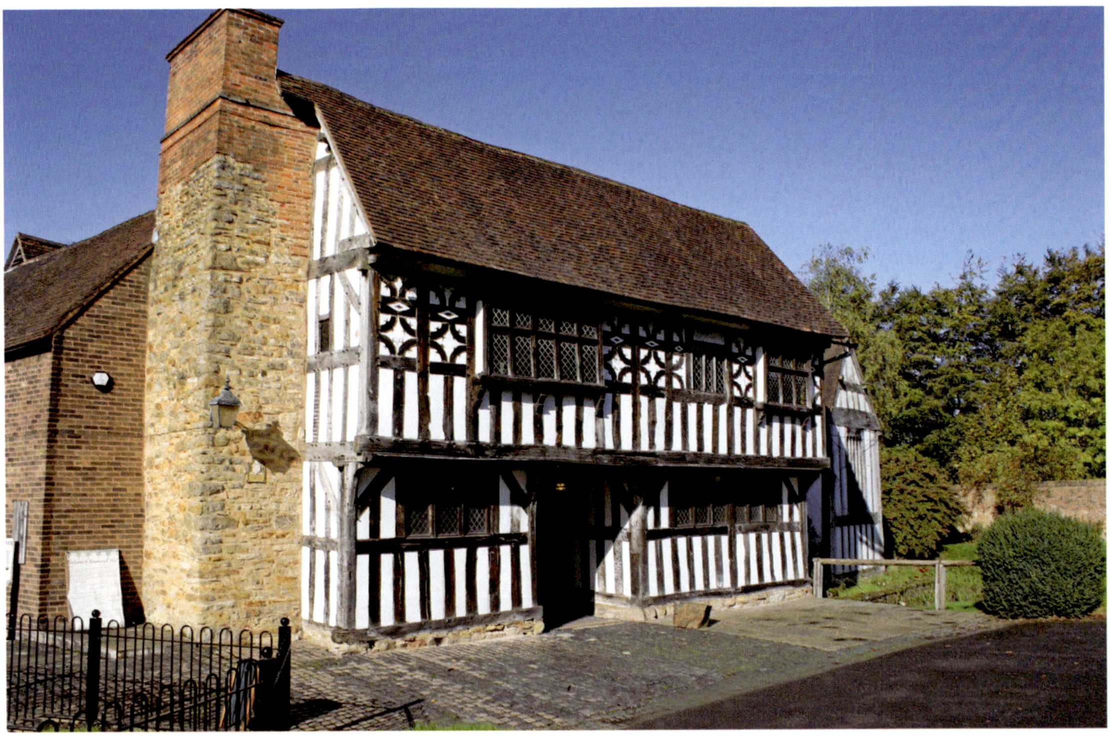

The main entrance of Bromwich Hall.

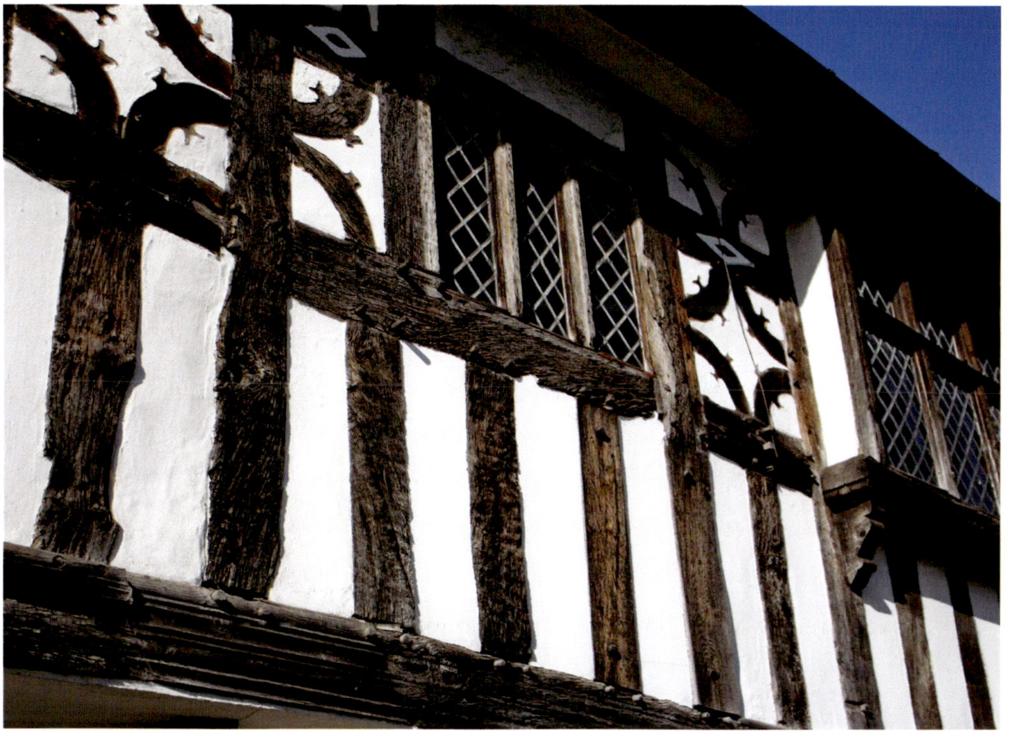

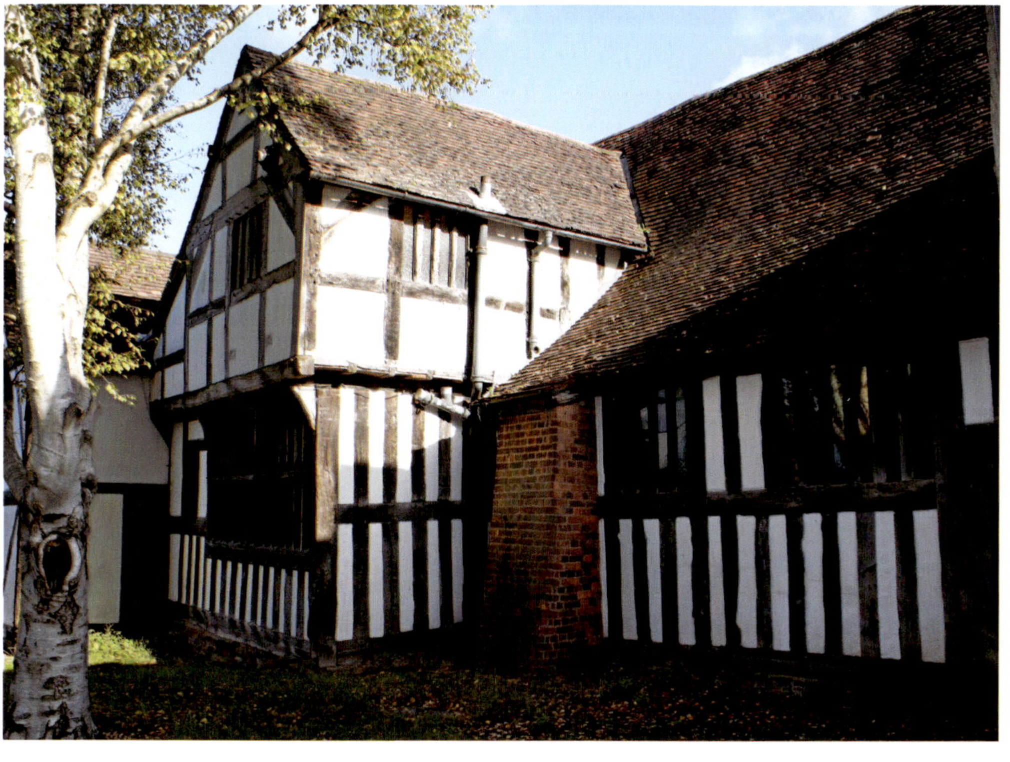

were converted into tenements. By the 1950s, Bromwich Hall was abandoned and deteriorated so badly that it faced demolition. Fortunately, it was saved at the last moment when the local council recognised the historical significance of the building they were about to lose.

In 1961, Bromwich Hall was given new lease of life when it was transformed into a prestigious pub and restaurant, The Manor House, attracting famous and influential customers from across the West Midlands. During this period, the ghosts of its past began manifesting more actively, surprising many with their varied appearances. Unseen forces reportedly hurled glass ashtrays across rooms, shattering them into countless pieces without any human presence. In one incident, a drunken patron, having consumed a few too many pints of ale, hurled verbal abuse at the staff. When the licensee, Pam, asked him to leave, and he refused, a pint glass mysteriously flew from a shelf behind the bar, striking and shattering against the man's shoulder. Upstairs, in what used to be a bar, guests frequently reported the sensation of a cat brushing against their legs, matching the description of one of the pub's long-deceased pets, yet saw nothing when they looked down at their feet. With these strange occurrences becoming more common, a team of paranormalists was invited in the 1980s for an overnight investigation. They set up tape recorders, capturing baseline

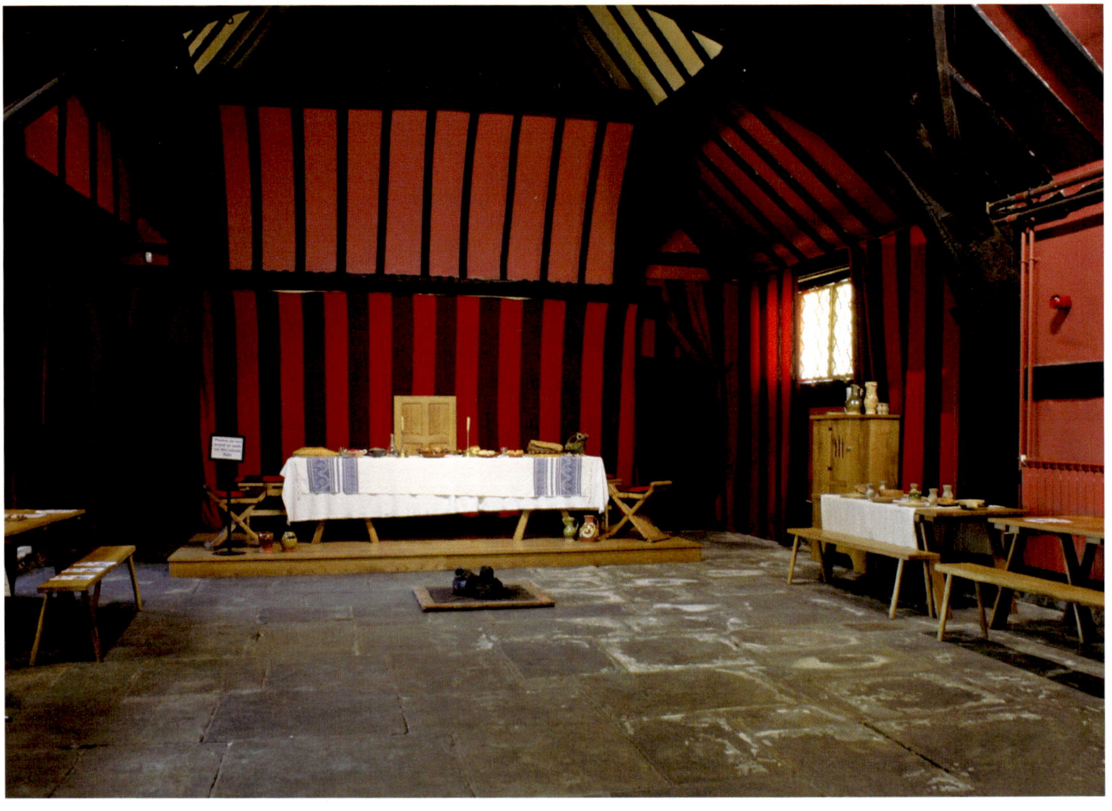

The large open space of the great hall is the oldest surviving part of the Bromwich Hall complex. Tree-ring dating has traced the timbers to between 1270–88, suggesting it could be the country's oldest example of this architectural feature.

sounds like their own footsteps, breathing, and nearby traffic for later comparison. However, as often happens in such investigations, nothing notable occurred until the early hours of the morning. One team member, feeling the fatigue of a long night, began reading a book when she suddenly felt a cold sensation on her nose. A minor but intriguing event, she described it to the tape recorders. Days later, while reviewing the recordings, the team heard children playing outside, timestamped at around four in the morning. More startlingly, when the recording of the lady describing the cold sensation was played back, a child's voice was heard saying, 'I know that,' followed by loud laughter.

Despite initial success, The Manor House pub faced a decline in patrons and closed in the 1990s, later becoming a museum maintained by Sandwell Council. During my visit, a volunteer enthusiastically told me about the building's rich history. When I inquired about any current ghostly occupants, she replied, 'Not that I'm aware of,' noting that most ghost stories dated from its pub days. However, she then recalled an incident where she and a colleague heard sounds resembling children playing in a small room behind the great hall. The two ladies investigated but found nothing in the room other than some stored-away furniture. She also mentioned another volunteer who, during a guided tour on the first floor, felt hands gripping her shoulders from behind. She quickly turned around in shock, only to find no one there.

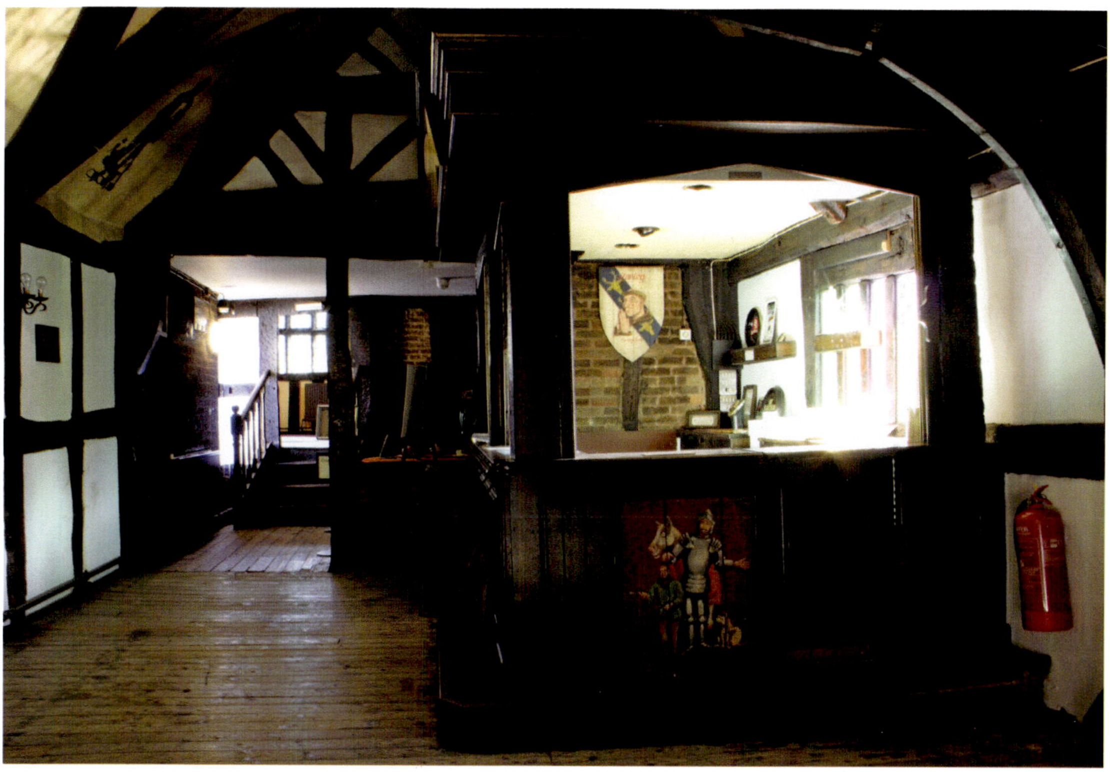

Although the pub closed many years ago, some features, such as the bar on the first floor, have been preserved.

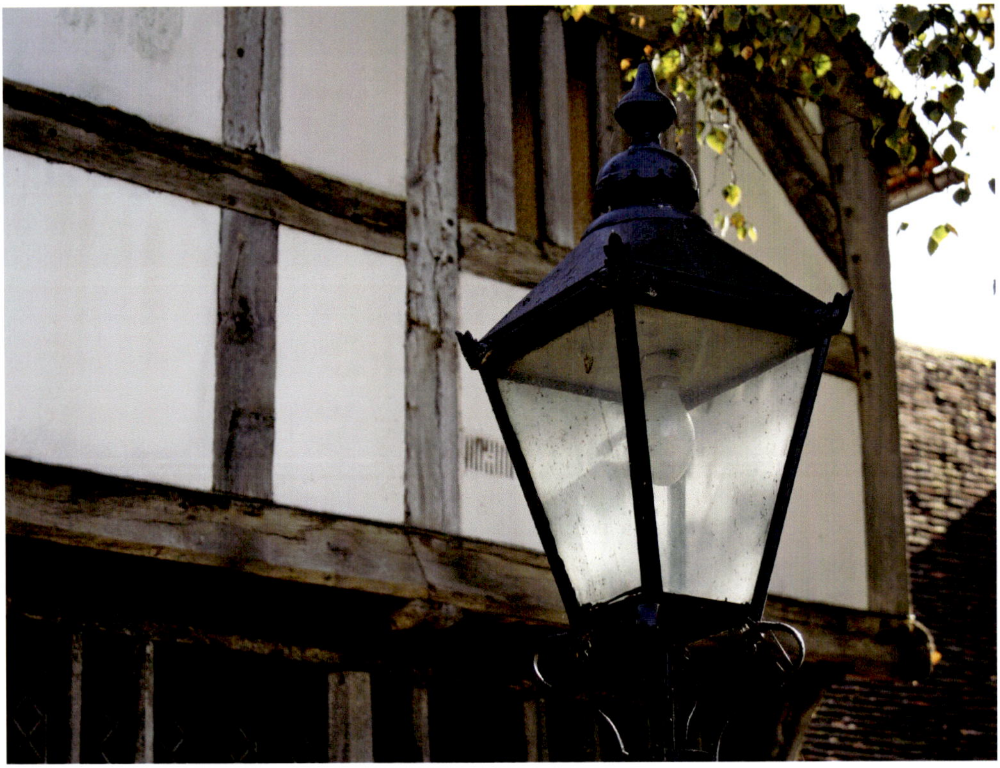

The Oak House

A short distance from the ancient Bromwich Hall stands another centuries-old, black-and-white timber-framed structure, surrounded by a starkly contrasting 1900s housing estate. Built around 1620 by yeoman farmers, it is roughly half the age of Bromwich Hall, but still plenty old enough to develop a reputation for hauntings, although some controversy exists around just how haunted it really is. While some insist it is void of ghosts, others, influenced by their experiences at the house, believe differently. Even the origins of its name are debated. The popular theory is that The Oak House was named after an oak tree that once stood in front of the building before meeting a fiery end in the early 1800s. This is contested by the museum, which maintains that, by the time the house was built, there were virtually no trees in Bromwich Heath. What is certain is that for most of its early existence, the Oak House served as a private residence for the Turton Family, who rose rapidly from farmers and ironmongers to wealthy gentry in the region.

The main entrance welcomes visitors into a large dining room, featuring large slab stone floors and a vast open fireplace, surrounded by oak-panelled walls and furniture that have absorbed the daily lives of its occupants over hundreds of years, echoing the images and conversations of family members. When the building is empty and quiet, the distant sound of a man and woman conversing can sometimes be heard, along with the tones of children singing, laughing, and playing in the corridors. The chimes

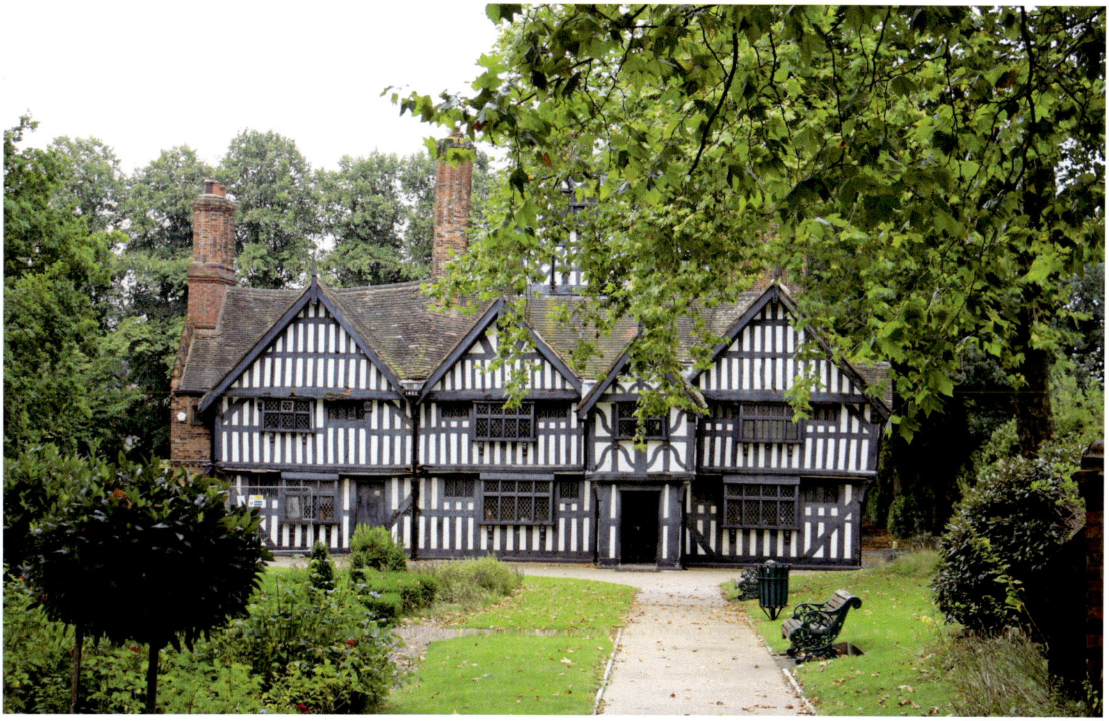

The Oak House, West Bromwich.

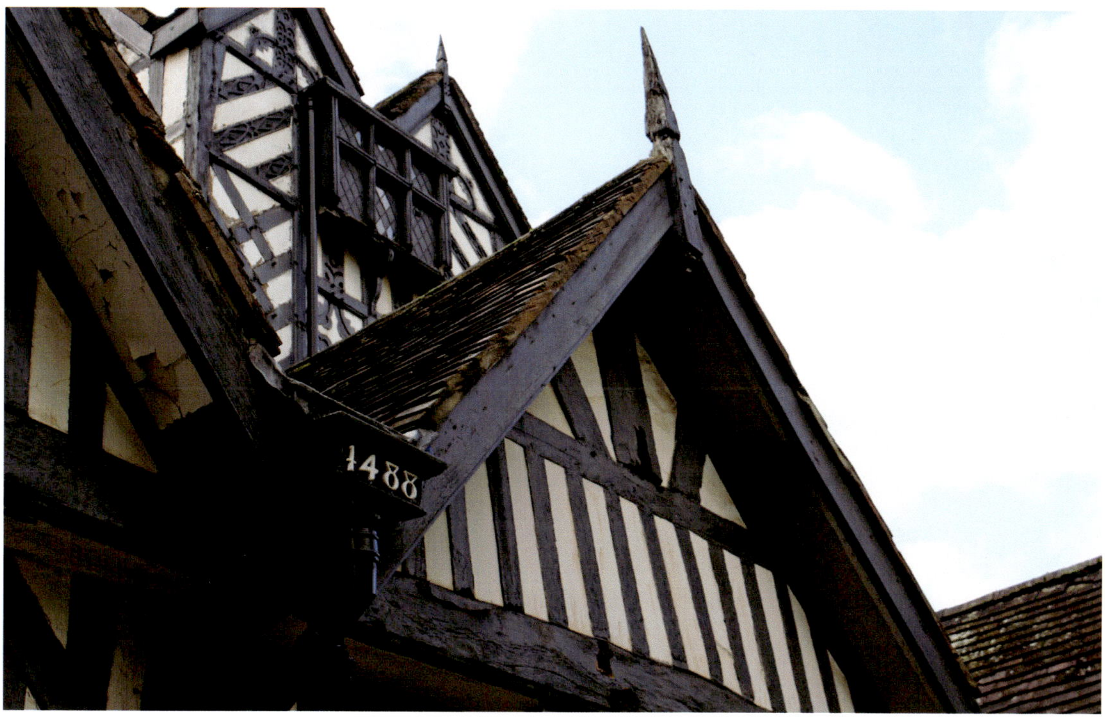

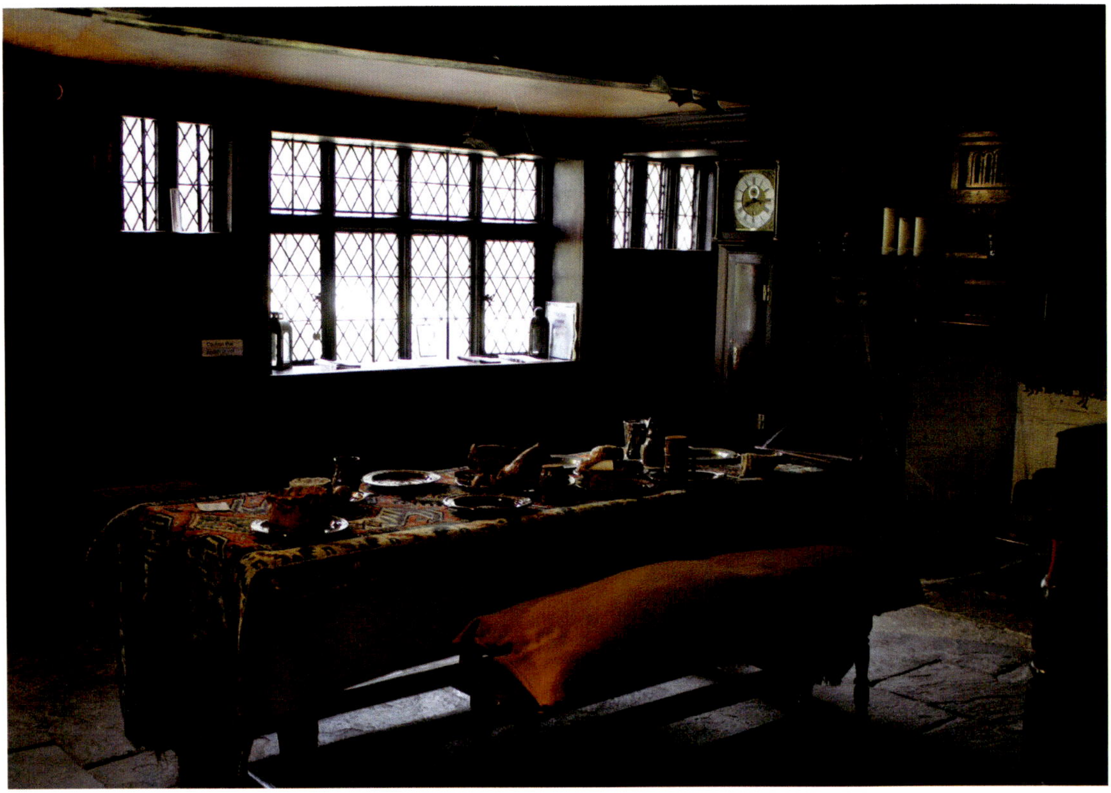

The atmospheric dining room is, as with most of the house, furnished to represent how it would have looked long ago. When I visited in October, a few cobwebs had been added by volunteers keen to get into the Halloween spirit.

of old, long-decommissioned clocks have also been heard by a few fortunate visitors in the living quarters. During my visit, one staff member told me how another volunteer, tidying up after the museum had closed, heard heavy footsteps pacing on the floorboards in the rooms above, but found the rooms to be empty when investigating.

The staircase to the first floor is also said to creak and groan under the weight of invisible footsteps, sometimes accompanied by glimpses of a child in old-fashioned clothing, seemingly vanishing into the walls. At the top of the staircase, in the front bedroom, a volunteer dusting furniture, while alone in the building, noticed a figure walking repeatedly past the doorway. Assuming it was her colleague, who had earlier disappeared briefly to pick up cleaned costumes from the local laundrette, she initially ignored it. Curiosity eventually compelled her to check, only to find that her colleague had not yet returned. In the same room, another visitor and her daughter described being so overwhelmed by a cold sensation that they were unable to move from where they stood for several minutes. On other occasions, children's dress-up clothes, tidied away, were found scattered across the floor moments later. On the ground floor, the kitchen is one of the most haunted areas. An old lady dressed in black has been seen glaring unwelcomingly at visitors from her seat in the corner. Assuming her to be a costumed volunteer, they complained about her sinister stare, only to learn later that no staff were dressed in black that day.

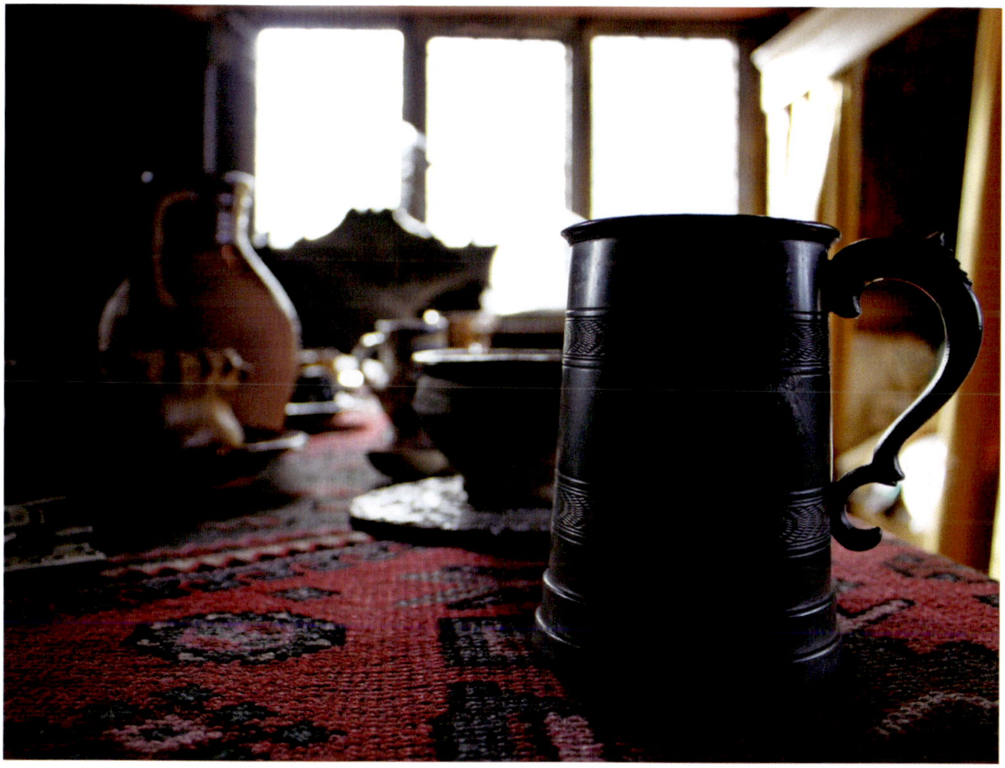

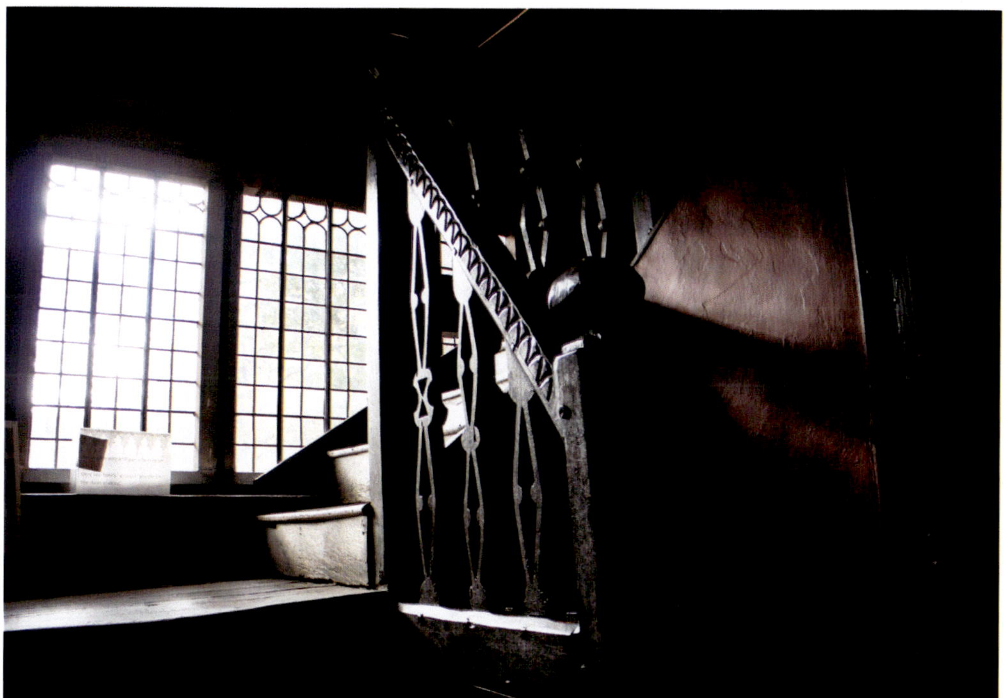

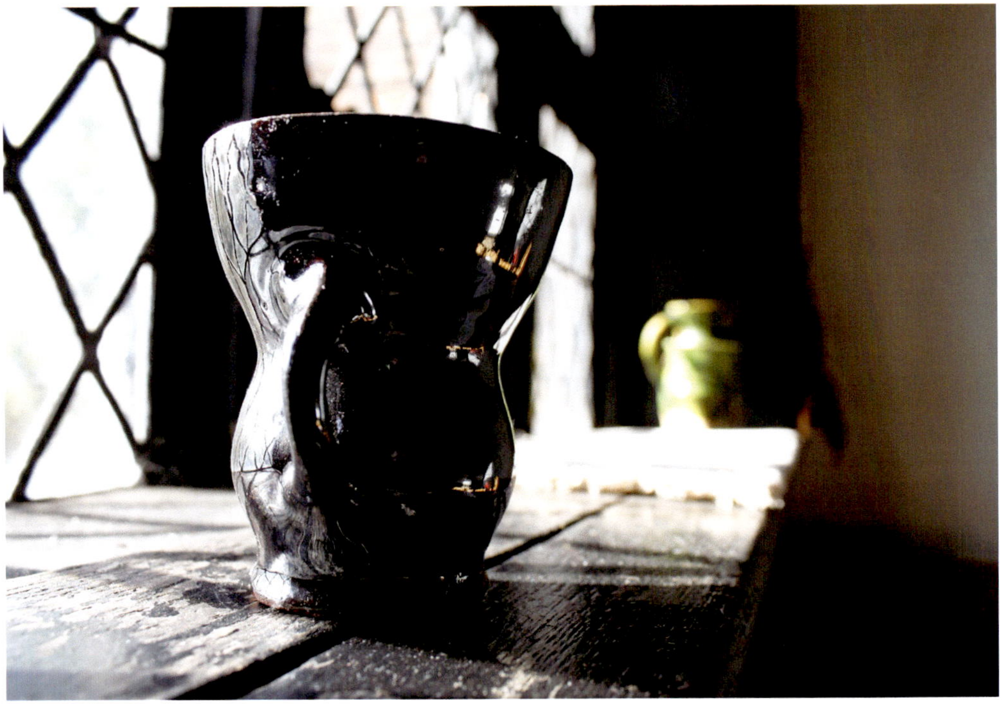

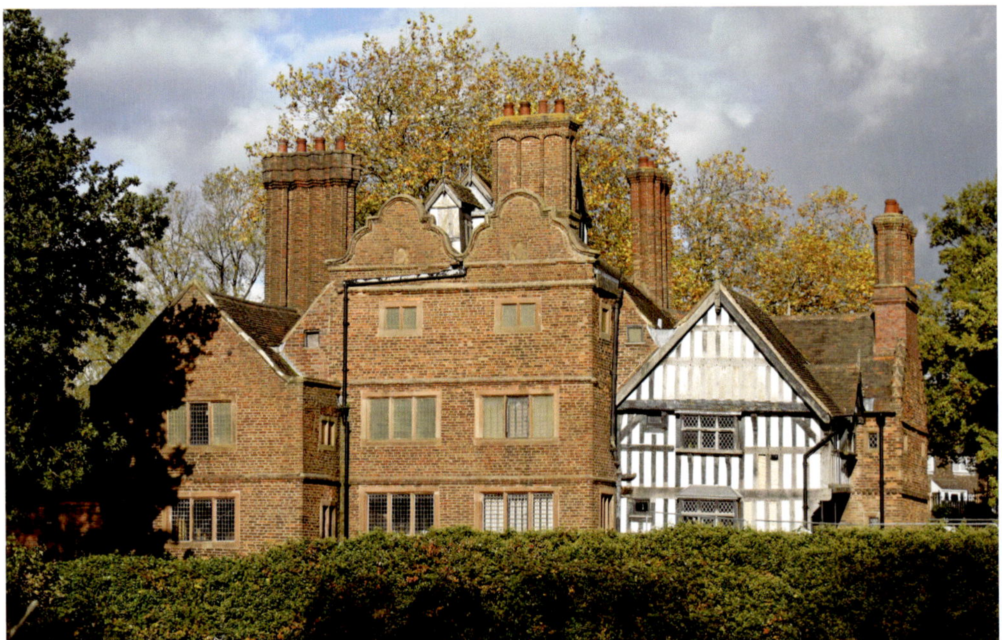

From the rear, the Oak House looks completely different. The brickwork structures were added in the 1650s and mainly used on the rear to preserve the character and charm of the original building when observed from the front.

Sandwell Priory

Shortly after midnight on a chilly November night in 1992, a lorry driver from nearby Bloxwich journeyed northward along the M5 in his truck. A thin scattering of clouds in the sky allowed the glow of a near-full moon to light the journey. As the road arced by the West Bromwich junction, the driver's gaze was drawn to a dark, hooded figure moving quickly down the embankment onto the carriageway. Instinctively, the driver punched the brake pedal with his right foot, and the tyres screeched in protest as the heavy lorry eventually ground to a halt. With his heart pounding and adrenaline surging through his body, the driver emerged from his

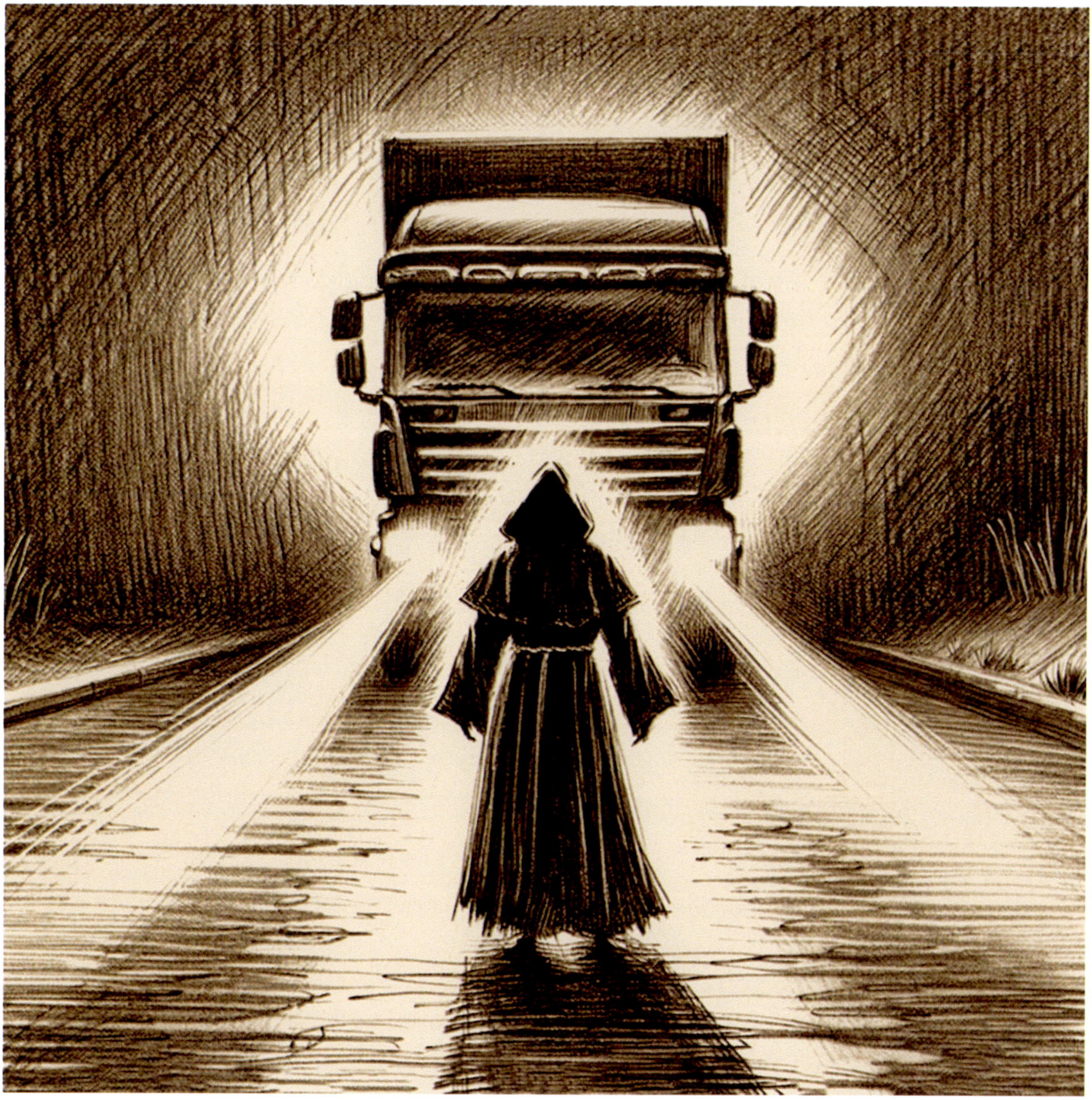

An ethereal encounter on the highway.

vehicle, certain he had struck the unfortunate figure. Yet, he found nothing but the empty darkness of the night. Concerned, the driver called the police to inform them of the incident, thinking the hooded figure might have fled the scene injured and in shock. The police quickly arrived, and a helicopter fitted with thermal imaging equipment roared overhead. Yet, despite searching through the night, no one was ever found. The following day, as journalists eagerly awaited their story, a motorway police spokesperson revealed to them that ghostly sightings of monks had been reported in the area for some years, but this was the first instance of them on the motorway.

The incident occurred on a stretch of motorway that runs through Sandwell Valley Country Park, only a few hundred meters from the ruins of Sandwell Priory, a Benedictine monastery founded in the late twelfth century. The motorway would seem more alien to the monks than the vivid green ring-necked parakeets noisily squawking in the treetops above the ruins today. But a path from the priory to West Bromwich would have once crossed the modern carriageway near where the phantom collision with the lorry driver in 1992 occurred. However, this isn't the only time a monk has been seen in the area. In 2016, police were alerted to another sighting of a hooded figure on the motorway, along with many similar stories reported over many years by people unfamiliar with the area's history.

The priory experienced a tumultuous history before its eventual decline, marked by bitter conflicts over land ownership, indiscipline among the monks, and poor integration with the local community. Eventually, the monastery was operating with only the prior and one monk. In 1525, an entire decade before Henry VIII's Dissolution of the Monasteries began, Sandwell Priory was dissolved as part of an initiative to finance a new college for Oxford University. After dissolution, much of the priory estate and property was sold off and later converted to a private dwelling known as Priory House. In the early eighteenth century, a large new Georgian house, Sandwell Hall, was built on the site, using some of the original foundations and masonry. Today, there is little more than a footprint of the original site, with a few walls poking up through the ground like a row of crooked teeth. As a scheduled monument, its remains are protected.

In early 1982, the *Sandwell Evening Mail* reported that a group of sixteen teenagers were about to embark on an architectural dig on the Sandwell site – the dig aimed to expose more of the foundations and look for other buried materials. The site already had a long reputation for monk sightings, and the town planning committee warned the group to be on the lookout for the shadowy spectres.

The phantom monks aren't tethered to the ruins themselves, as reports of their sightings cover the entire country park. Motorists have also reported seeing dark hooded figures crossing the road on the nearby junction one roundabout, on which an arched building stands that was once part of the entrance to the estate of Sandwell Hall. The island is also associated with a lady dressed in white, who is often spotted in the early hours of the morning. When motorists stop, assuming she is a hitchhiker or lost, she disappears almost immediately. In at least one case, when a motorist stopped, she climbed into the car's back seats and asked the driver to take her to Heath Lane cemetery to see her sister. The driver quickly felt an intense cold, and when they looked in their rearview mirror, she let out a loud shriek before vanishing suddenly.

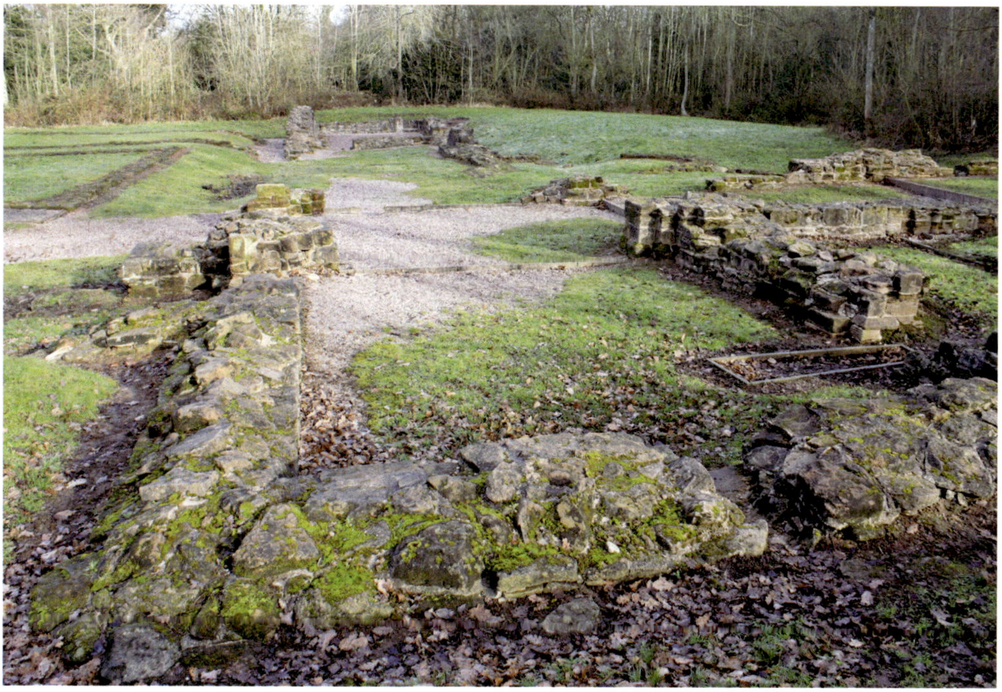

The ruins provide clues as to the priory's original layout, including the church with at least two tombs and outlines of a cloister, stables, and living spaces.

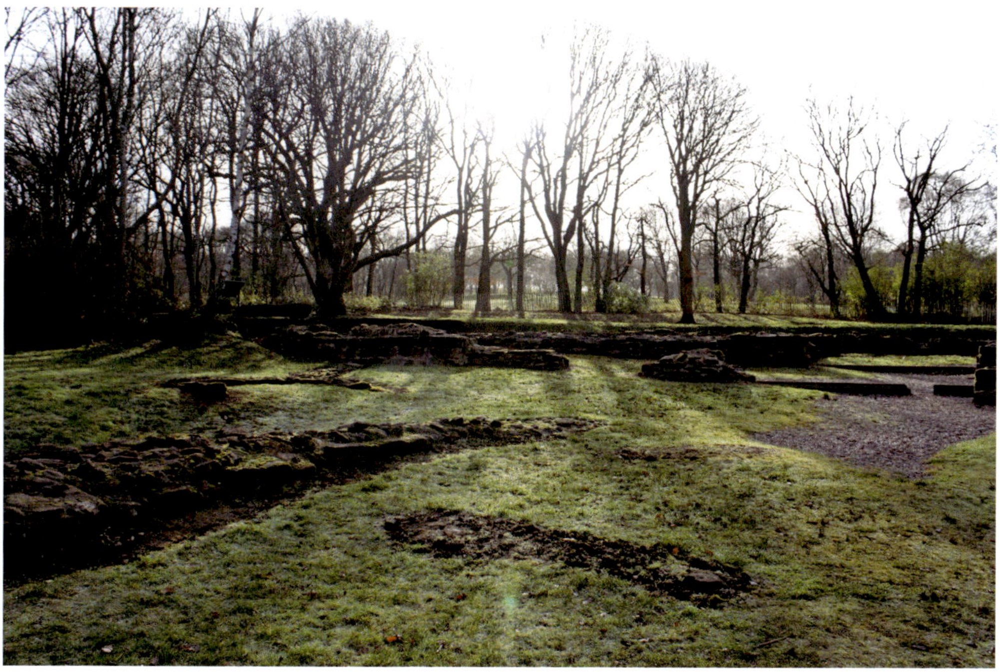

Sandwell Priory ruins.

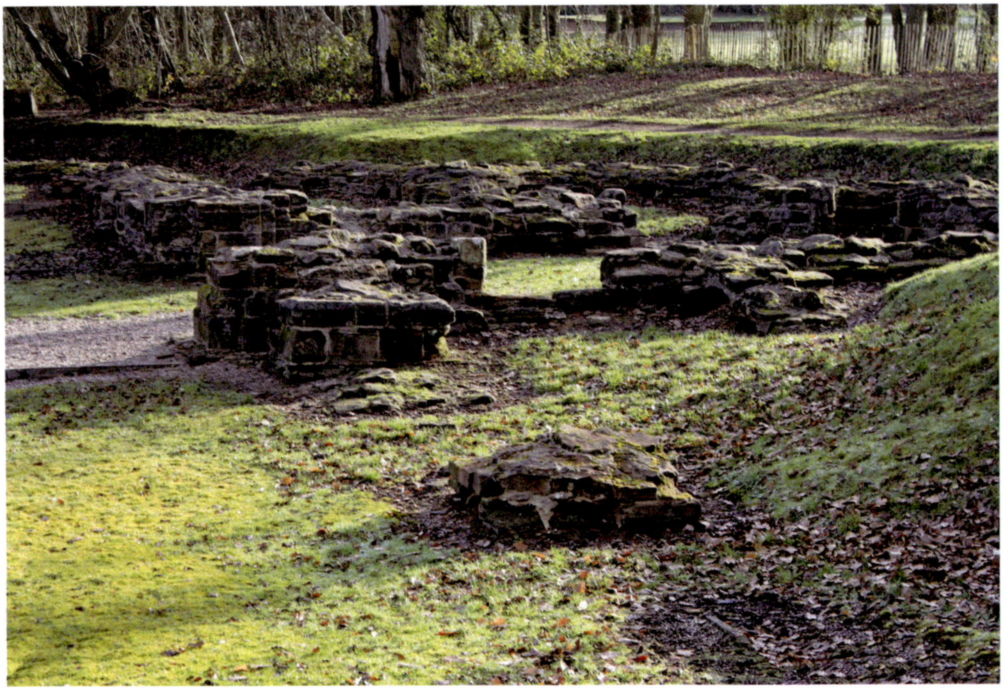

Sandwell Priory ruins.

Nearby Wasson Pool, better known as Swan Pool, is a former millpool with a spooky reputation. Many people have reported seeing a white figure silently moving across the water's surface, and while many say it's just one of the pool's many resident swans, witnesses dispute this. One user in an online discussion forum described their sightings of the figure as, 'a wavy white shape floating about in the dark and nearly always at tree top level'.

In 1999, a different kind of sighting caused a significant commotion within the local community and eventually gained national attention. In March, a group of anglers reported seeing a creature approximately 3 feet long, with a lengthy snout and tail. The local council received at least six similar reports in quick succession, and remains of a mangled pike were discovered in the pool. As unlikely as it may have been, the possibility of it being an escaped alligator led to the pool's closure for anglers and watersports enthusiasts. Over the following weekend, more than 8,000 people travelled from all over the country to visit the pool, hoping to catch a glimpse of the creature, dubbed the 'Valleygator'. This group included alligator hunters equipped with torches and specialised gear, who conducted searches throughout the night. Local reptile experts believed it was more likely a non-native cayman, a member of the crocodile family. By the following week, the creature was suspected to be a North American salamander instead, released by an owner who could no longer care for it. With no further sightings, the pool was eventually reopened. In the following days, a snapping turtle was spotted sunbathing on the pool's edge, nicknamed by locals as the Sandwell Snapper.

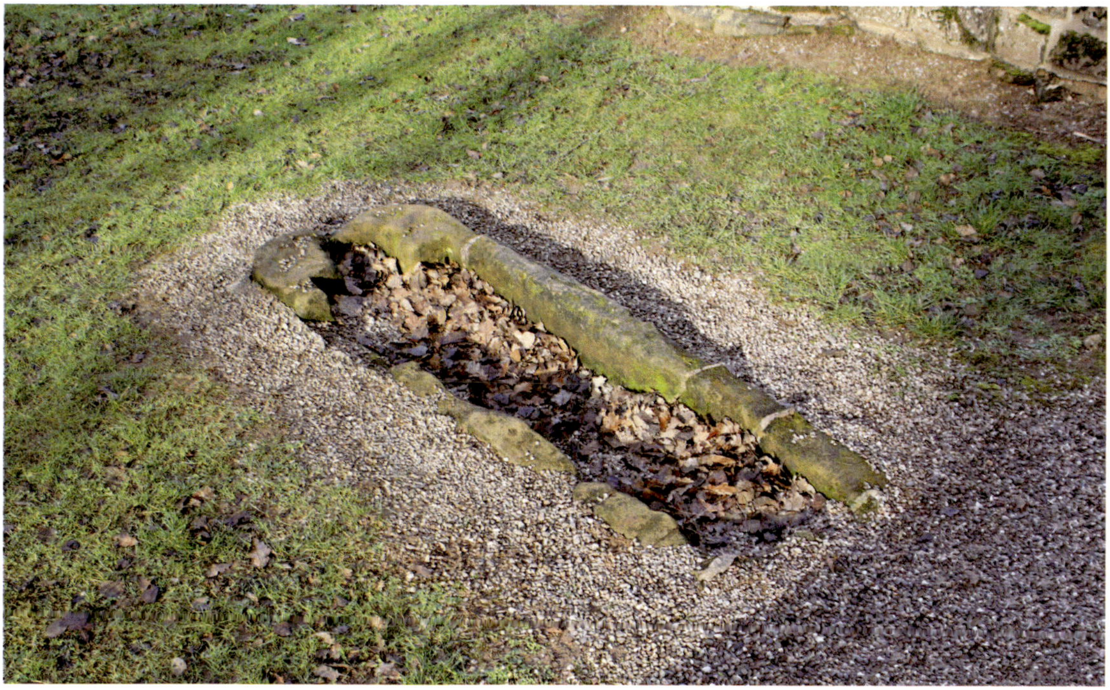

Sandwell Priory ruins.

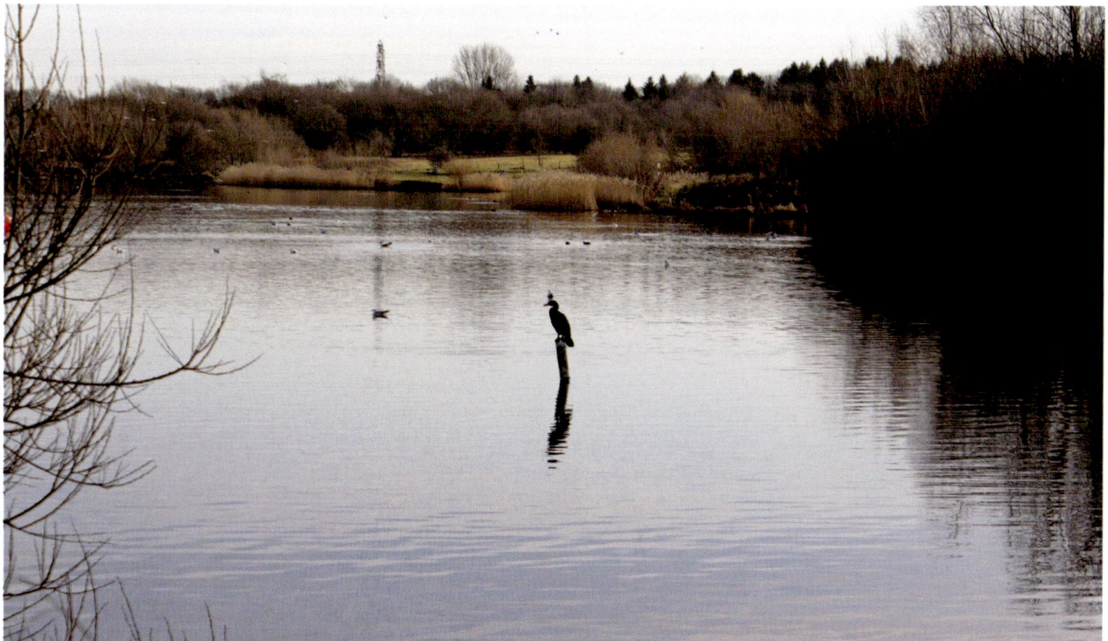

Along with snapping turtles and possibly an alligator, the pool is also home to a stunning array of birdlife.

Walsall

Regarded during the industrial era as a centre for metalworking, blacksmiths in Walsall produced some of the finest horse stirrups, bits, and braces. Yet, this town also harbours unusual mysteries that add an intriguing layer to its historical narrative. In 1972, renovation works were being carried out on a former Masonic Hall in Freer Street, when foreman Tony Dudley encountered what he believed was the ghost of a teenage girl during a final walk around of the building before work began. His colleagues initially dismissed the encounter, suggesting nothing more than a reflection from a large mirror or window blinds moving in the wind. However, their scepticism waned when the renovation uncovered gravestones hidden behind the wallpaper. Among them was a marker for an eighteen-year-old girl who died in 1834. 'We were all sceptical when Tony said he had seen a ghost,' said colleague Brian Ireston, 'But since we uncovered the tombs, we are tending to believe him after all.'

A few years later, in Newport Street, the sceptical owner of the Starting Gate pub was also beginning to experience a shift in his scepticism. Barry Vincent was originally a non-believer, dismissing rumours as pub gossip, but told the *Walsall Observer* in 1983 that too many things had happened for him to overlook. Glasses would inexplicably fly off shelves, lager taps seemed to turn on by themselves, and patrons reported feeling an icy touch on their shoulders when no one was nearby. But one pub in Walsall is shrouded in mystery and hauntings, which have become firmly embedded in local folklore.

White Hart Inn

The White Hart Inn of Caldmore Green, a building steeped in mystery and rich with paranormal lore, rose to notoriety in the nineteenth century after a chilling discovery in its shadowy attic. Known as one of the Black Country's most haunted locales, its history is as intriguing as it is eerie.

Built in the seventeenth century on the site of an earlier manor house, the White Hart initially served as the home of Walsall's mayor, George Hawe, before becoming an inn in 1801. Things took a dark turn in 1870 when renovation work uncovered a startling find in the attic. Buried beneath centuries of dust and dirt, a child's mummified arm was found lying beside a Cromwellian-era sword. Many speculated that the arm was a Hand of Glory, a gruesome relic of witchcraft believed to possess supernatural powers.

Traditionally, the creation of a Hand of Glory involved a macabre process: severing an arm from a hanged felon and preserving it in various salts until completely dried.

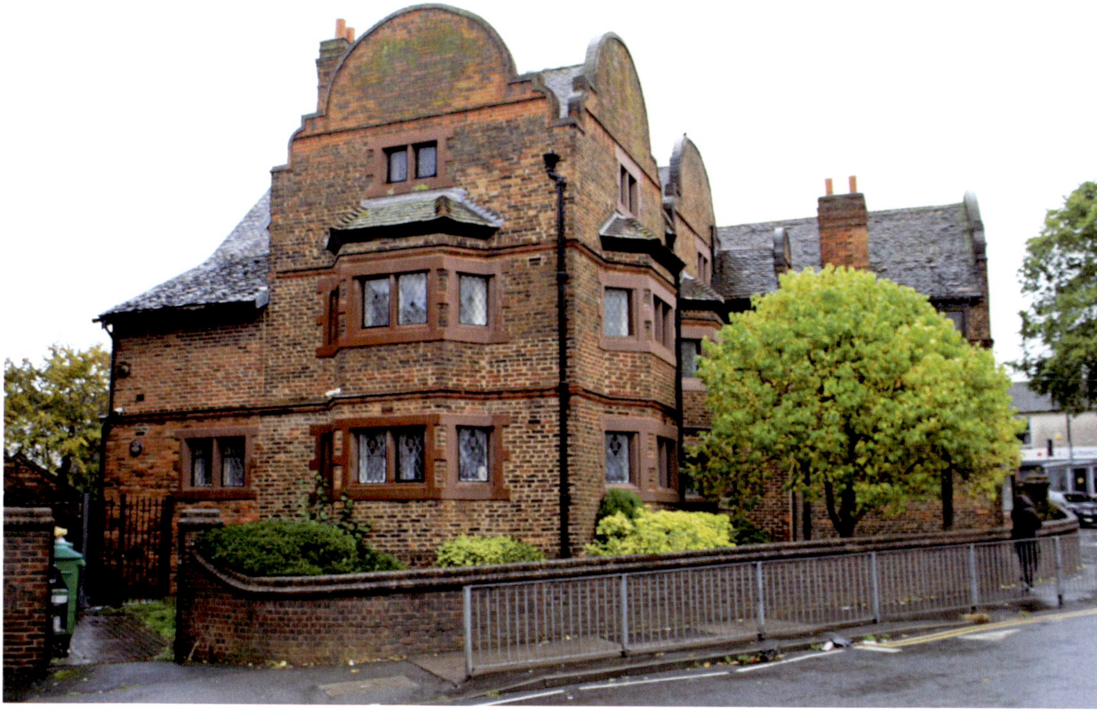

The White Hart Inn, Walsall's oldest brick building, stands on a busy junction surrounded by bustling shops and modern homes.

The arm would then be fashioned into a candle using the felon's own fat, blended with virgin wax and Lapland sesame. Burglars of old times held a superstitious belief that lighting this gruesome candle would paralyse the inhabitants of a house, enabling them to plunder without interruption. A 1965 study by Birmingham University's medical school, however, suggested the arm was more likely a mummified medical specimen.

Despite this mundane conclusion, the morbid discovery provided the fuel for numerous ghostly White Hart tales. Many of the stories stemmed from the alleged suicide of a servant girl in the attic in the late 1800s, leading to reports of eerie sounds, spectral sightings, and mysterious handprints in the dust. Helena Jones, who resided in the building in the late 1940s with her husband, the then licensee, vividly recalled waking up to an uninvited visitor by her bed. 'Once, I awoke early with an uneasy feeling,' recalled Mrs Jones. 'As I opened my eyes, I saw a white form shimmering by my bed.' Helena was too terrified to do anything other than dive under the bedsheets and hope the ethereal figure would leave. Although she only witnessed the apparition once, she frequently heard unsettling noises, including the, 'Clomp, Clomp, Clomp of footsteps!' Ascending the wooden stairs and passing by her bedroom door. 'My hair was in curlers, but it stood right up on end,' said Mrs Jones.

She felt something strange about the White Hart Inn that was, 'Hard to explain', and always had the impression that someone was watching her. Mrs Jones and her husband avoided speaking about it so as not to frighten their children. Yet, their silence could not shield their eldest daughter from unsettling noises emanating from the attic. These sounds, usually heard around 3 a.m., often resembled a series of bumps, disturbing her sleep in the quiet of the night.

During his tenure as the licensee in the 1950s, James Moran often recounted his experiences of hearing peculiar sounds during the night, emanating from the attic above. Upon investigation, he once found a small imprint of a woman's hand, as if grasping the edge of a table. This was particularly unsettling since the table was stored away in the attic, a place long untouched by the living. Joan, his wife, often disturbed by thumping sounds from the loft, shared his unease These noises also alarmed their dogs, who would growl and stare intently at the heavy oak door separating them from whatever lurked in the attic.

In 1955, A former RAF policeman, James Paxton, worked as a relief manager at the inn. While in the living quarters, on the floor below the haunted attic, Mr Paxton heard noises: 'It was like someone slowly pacing the floor of the loft,' recalled James. He looked towards the door, which was slightly ajar. By it, a large Alsatian who lived at the inn stood stiff, its fur bristling on its back, staring up the stairs towards the loft. 'That was enough for me,' said Mr Paxton. 'I ran downstairs as fast as my legs would carry me.'

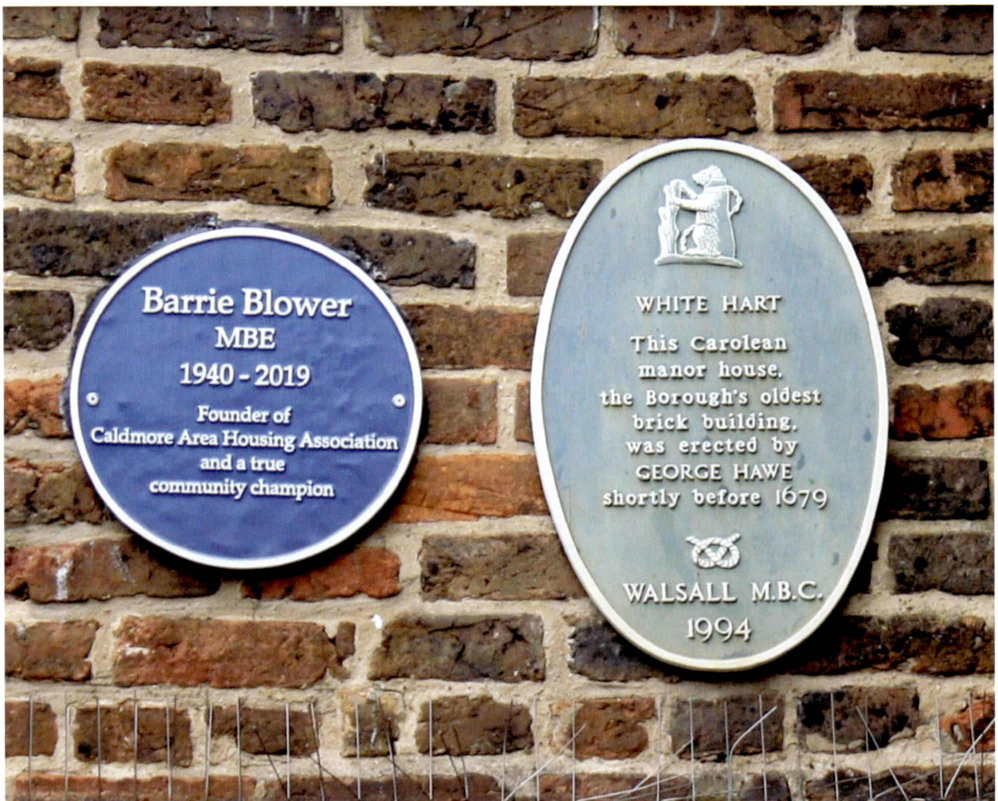

Before becoming an inn, the White Hart was the home of George Hawe, the town's mayor, who is commemorated with a plaque on the building next to Barrie Blower MBE.

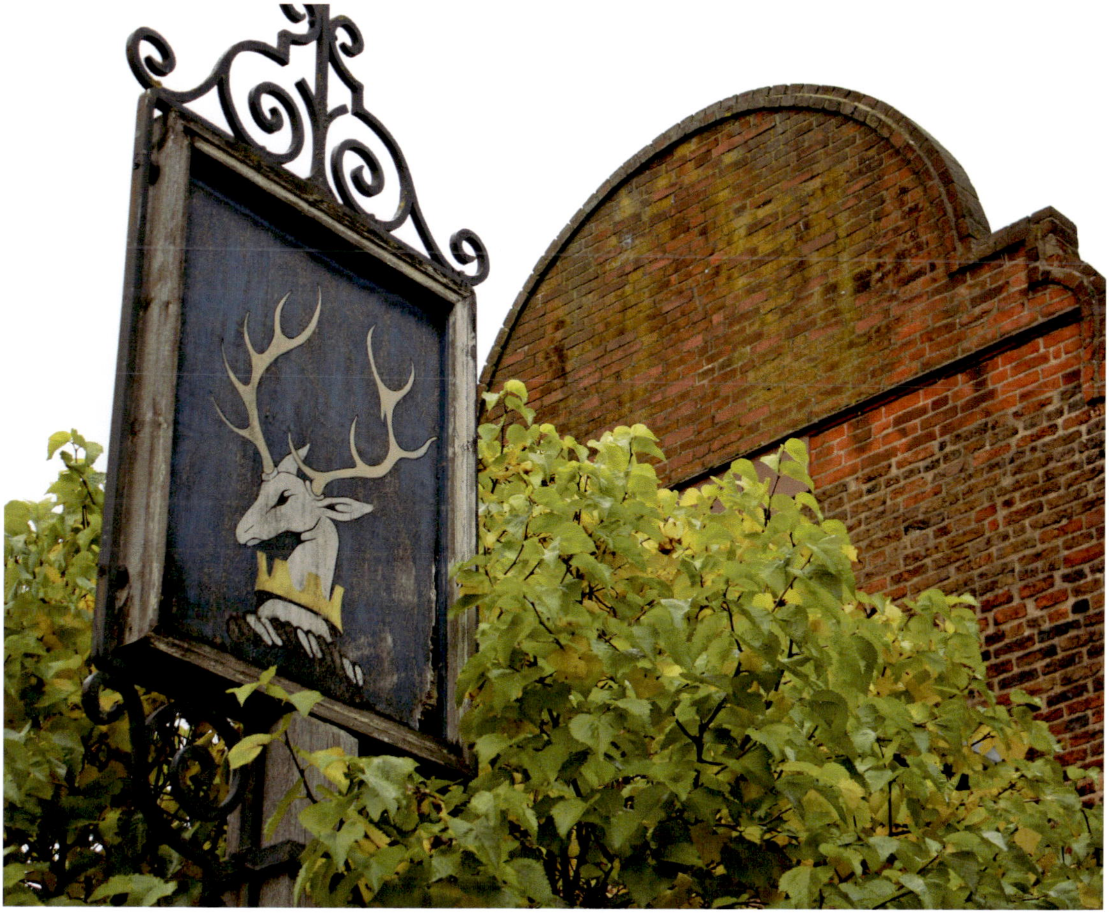

Although now converted to private residences, symbols of its hostelry past remain.

As years passed, the White Hart Inn's reputation evolved, becoming known less for its ghosts and more for its rough and rowdy atmosphere, where fights were common. Some patrons humorously blamed the ghosts for serving 'mad beer', which allegedly caused temporary insanity and scraps between the customers. Eventually, the pub closed down, and in the 1990s, the building was transformed into apartments. It seems that as the bar and pub furnishings were stripped away, so too were the ghosts, and mentions of their haunts diminished. The White Hart Inn's ghosts may have retreated into the shadows, but their legacy will endure in local folklore for decades to come.

Mossley Estate

When Leonard Ayres moved into his new home on Shrewsbury Close in the Mossley Estate in 1976, it seemed an idyllic place to raise a family with his wife, Julie, and their eight-year-old son. But a few months after settling in, an unearthly visitor triggered the first of many visitations, casting a chilling darkness throughout their once cosy home. One evening, Leonard was sitting in his front room when the hazy figure of an old woman dressed in white appeared before him. Her ethereal figure manifested in the doorway and floated across the room, disappearing through a wall. As unsettling as this experience may have been for Leonard, he decided it was best not to tell his wife to avoid causing unnecessary worry. After all, it might have been a one-off. And it seemed that way for some time until his wife, Julie, woke to the vision of a mysterious dark figure in their bedroom. She quickly shook Leonard awake, exclaiming, 'Look, there's someone in the room!' He thought she was dreaming until he saw it, too, a few moments later. 'I hadn't seen anything since the day I saw the old woman in white three years ago,' Leonard recalled. He described the apparition as a man dressed in

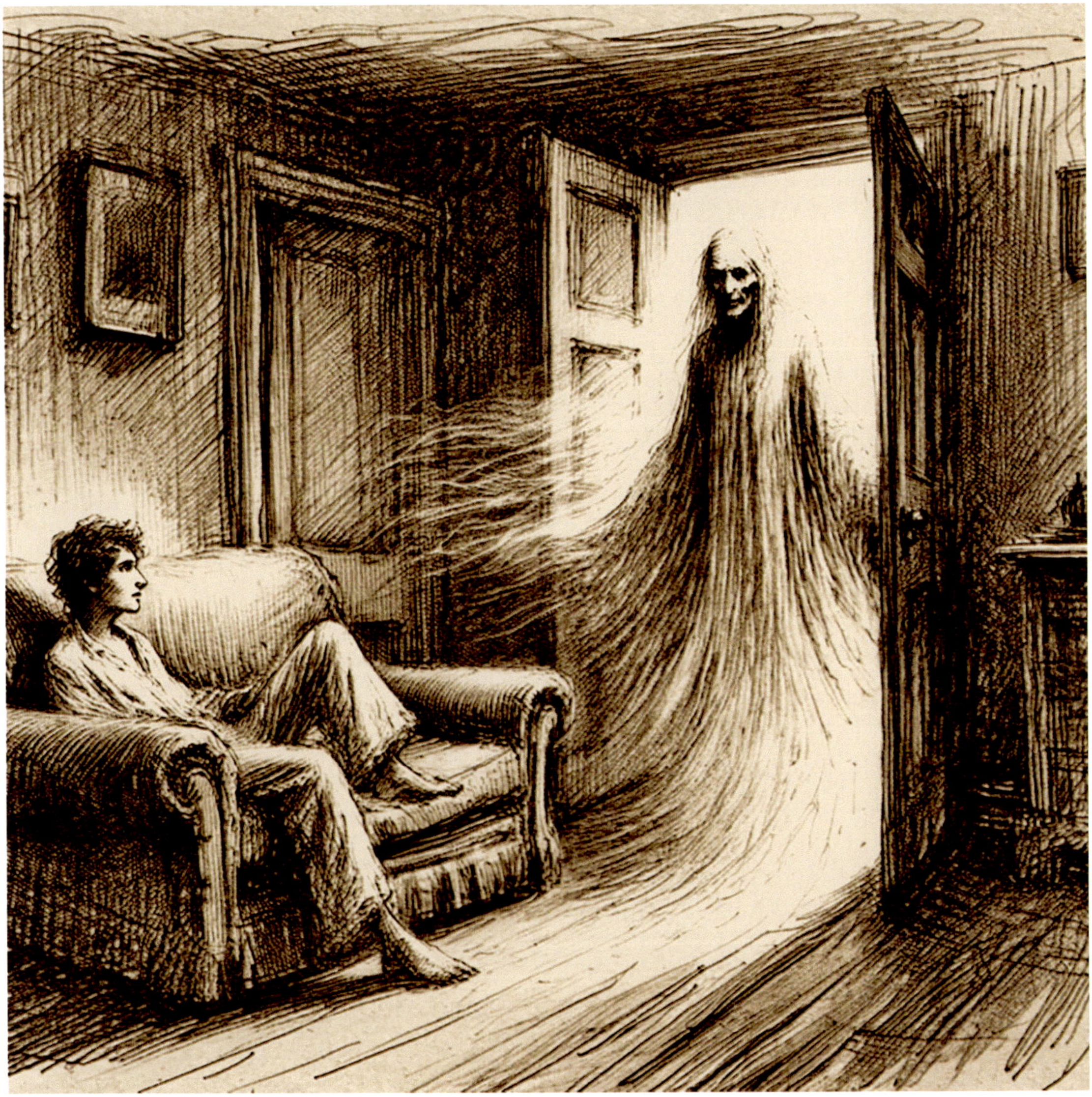

Leonard's first encounter with the ghost of Mossley Estate.

a long, black robe with a rope knotted around his waist, floating slowly from the bedroom door to the window before drifting back across the room and melting away through the door.

Little did they know, but this was only the beginning of a series of terrifying visitations, including the return of the old woman in white, roaming various parts of the house, and a miner, blackened with coal dust from a long day underground. A mysterious black cat also began appearing in the living room alongside the family's pets. Even when the ghosts were unseen, the sound of their footsteps echoed at any time, day or night, and an unfamiliar scent of perfume lingered in some rooms.

In an attempt to rid the house of their otherworldly guests, Leonard sought help from local churchmen, hoping for an exorcism. Revd Joe Edwards, the vicar of All Saints Church, noted that such activity had been reported more frequently since the release of the film *The Exorcist*, suggesting it played on people's minds. 'So often, these ghosts are not in people's houses, but in their imaginations,' the reverend remarked. Despite the churchmen performing prayers of exorcism, the ghosts persisted. Spiritualists who visited the house reported it as being overwhelmed with spirits. 'What we registered were phenomena connected to a time long past,' stated Mrs Brenda Benton, president of Bloxwich Spiritualist Church, who, along with two colleagues, had visited the Ayres' home. She observed that while the Ayres family seemed particularly sensitive to these phenomena, something in the house was 'not pleasant at all'.

The increasing frequency and intensity of the sightings began to wear heavily on the family, disrupting their sleep and raising constant concerns for their young son's safety. Left with no other option, they decided to move in with Leonard's mother. 'We're at our wits' end and just don't know what to do,' Leonard expressed. When this story was first reported in the *Walsall Observer* in April 1981, a housing transfer for the family was urgently being processed.

The Weeping Lady of Bloxwich

Before the construction of the M6 and other major infrastructure in the area, the tiny village of Bloxwich lay on the main route between Walsall and Cannock, making it an ideal location for a coaching inn, where tales of legends were shared over beer tankards for decades. One such legend dates back to the 1720s.

Like a bad cliché, the story takes place on a wild, stormy night in the middle of winter. Powerful gales blasted icy air against the carriages of travellers making their perilous journey along the Stafford road. A large snow drift formed in a natural hollow in the road, rendering it impassable. Among the stranded coaches was one containing a young woman carrying a roll of purple French silk, an expensive commodity at the time. The nearest shelter was the Old King's Arms in Wallington Heath, where she and other weary travellers found lodging for the night, while the coachmen and ostlers recovered in cottages opposite the inn. The wind howled throughout the night, but by morning, the tempest had eased into a manageable breeze. However, the travellers awoke to a different kind of storm.

As they gathered for breakfast, it became apparent that one guest was missing: the girl with the French silk. Also absent was one of the ostlers. Fearing the worst, a search was launched, and it wasn't long before their fears were confirmed. In one of the upper-floor rooms of the inn, they found the mutilated body of the young lady. Her throat had been slit, and her right hand, likely removed to steal her jewellery, was missing. The young lady's struggle and agonising cries would have been drowned out by the raging storm outside. The prime suspect for this despicable act was the ostler, who had taken a horse and was long gone.

Following this tragedy, the figure of the weeping lady was said to appear on every stormy night, sitting beneath an ash tree by the pool near the inn. Some believe her spirit lingered at the King's Arms, weeping for her missing silk. Others tell of her

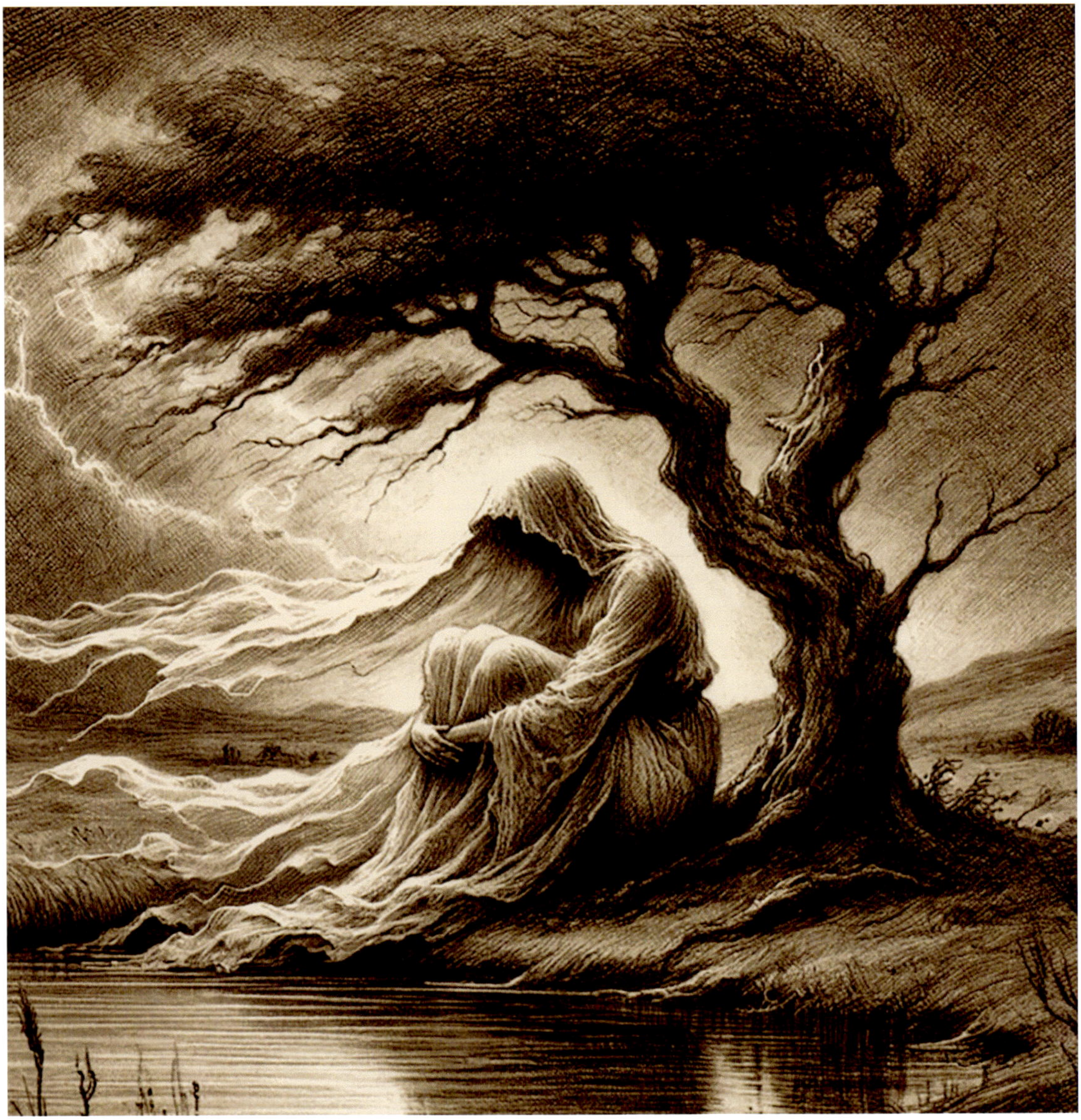

The weeping lady of Bloxwich.

outline appearing on the yellow-plastered wall of the inn abutting the road, which continued to reappear despite being plastered over many times.

In the early 1900s, the inn was converted into a French convent of nuns, where the lady's spirit appears to have finally found peace, as the sightings ceased.

The Flying Nun

From this period emerged another apparition, known locally as the Flying Nun or the Grey Lady of Bloxwich. The nun, believed to have drowned herself in the shallow, boggy waters of the pool beside the convent, appeared in contrast to the weeping lady. She was sometimes seen on clear, moonlit nights, floating peacefully above the water's

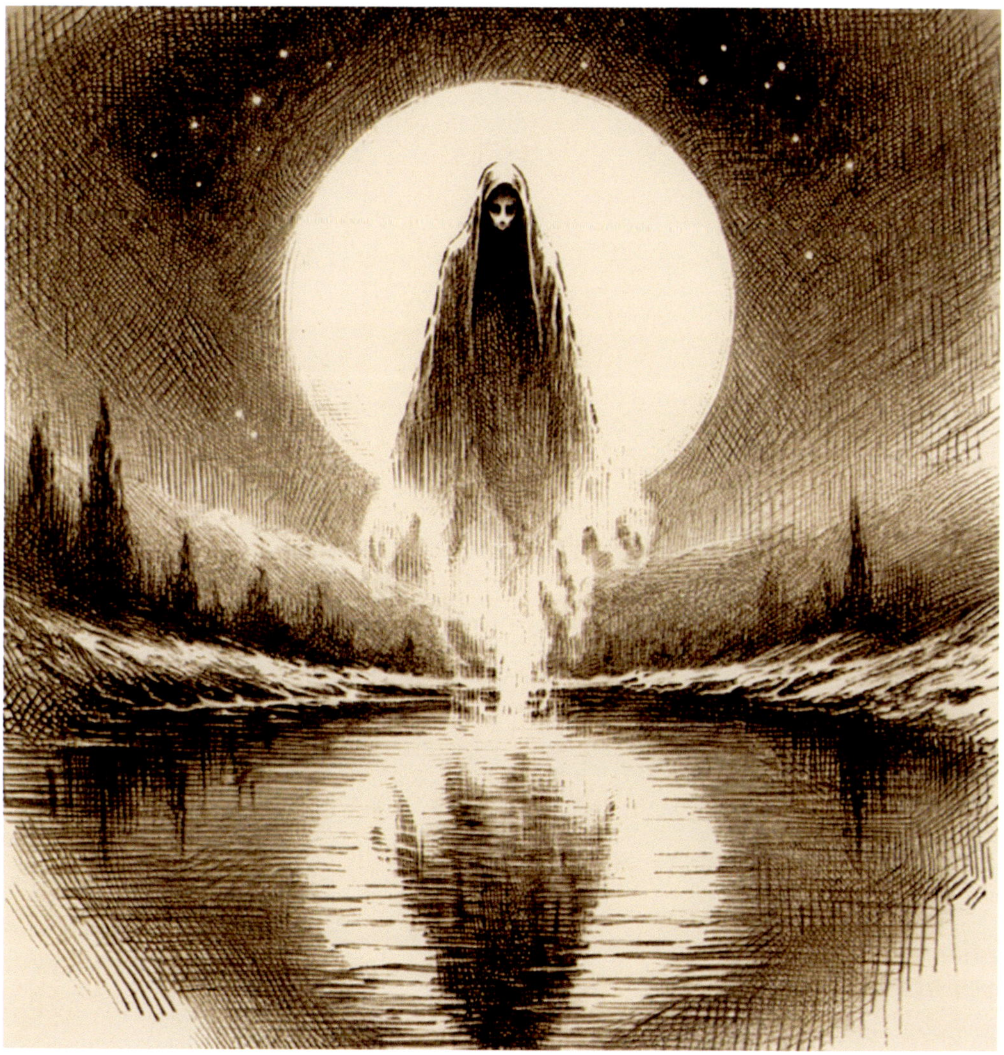

The legend of the flying nun was sighted as recently as 2014.

surface. Although sightings were rare, in 2014, a Bloxwich local shared on social media his father's experience. He recounted his father driving along Stafford Road late one night towards Bloxwich when he saw a woman in a nun's habit sitting under one of the trees opposite where the convent used to stand before its demolition in the 1960s. As he drove past, he watched the nun vanish into thin air.

Sleepwalking by the Pool

One of the most peculiar experiences was shared with me by Kate Gould, a Bloxwich resident. She recalled her young nephew Daryl's strange behaviour in the late 1960s. Daryl, around eight or nine years old at the time, lived in a newly built house on Lydford Road. The convent had closed in 1964, but the buildings and pool were still present and a short walk from Daryl's house. One night, Daryl's mother, Yvonne, noticed he was missing from his bedroom. She found the back door of the house unlocked and open, and eventually discovered Daryl sitting by the edge of the pool, wide-eyed but asleep. Yvonne, a nurse, knew it was best not to wake a sleepwalker, so she gently guided him back to his room. Daryl had no previous history of sleepwalking but repeated the behaviour several times over the following weeks, always ending up at the pool and mumbling to himself. One night, Yvonne followed him to the water's edge and tapped him on the shoulder, asking, 'Daryl, what are you doing?' He quickly shushed his mother and whispered, 'I'm talking with the lady in black.'

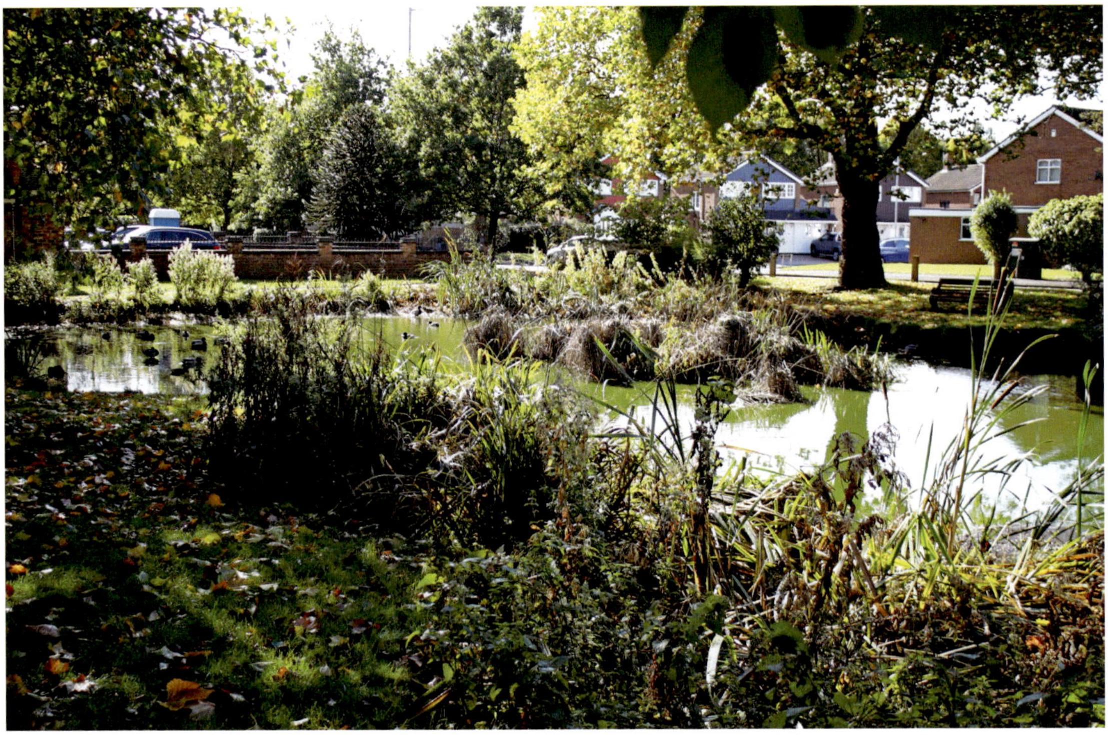

The inn and convent are now long gone, with a few small pools the only part that remains.

The Haunted Farms of Bloxwich

Less than a mile from the site of St Paul's Convent lies Hills House Farm. Built in 1682, the farm has been the home of many generations of farming families. In 1970, the Roe family shared their experiences from their twenty-four years living in the ancient farmhouse.

From their first night in the farmhouse, the Roes realised they weren't alone. Mrs Florence Roe recounted that her husband's sisters, who stayed with them during that first night, slept in the same room. 'They were woken by the sound of someone shuffling around the bed,' Mrs Roe recalled, 'but they were too terrified to open their eyes.' Other family members often heard similar sounds when they were downstairs. Each time, they searched for a logical explanation. 'We rushed upstairs to see if we had burglars,' Mrs Roe said after hearing the sounds, but they never found anyone.

As time passed, the noisy presence began to manifest as shadows passing by the living room window. Gradually, the family grew accustomed to these spooky experiences. They came to believe that, even if they shared the house with something supernatural, it had never harmed anyone, so they had no reason to fear it.

Nearby, another farm was reputedly haunted by the ghost of a nurse. The haunting began with the sounds of footsteps on the stairs and heavy doors swinging open without explanation. Although the owner at the time, Mr Sid Downes, had never seen the ghost himself, many others claimed they had. 'One lady who lives in a bungalow overlooking the farm drive has seen me walking up the drive followed by a woman wearing a long cloak,' Sid recounted, aware that there should have been no one else there. He added that his mother also saw the figure of a woman dressed in a nurse's outfit standing at the foot of her bed when she stayed overnight.

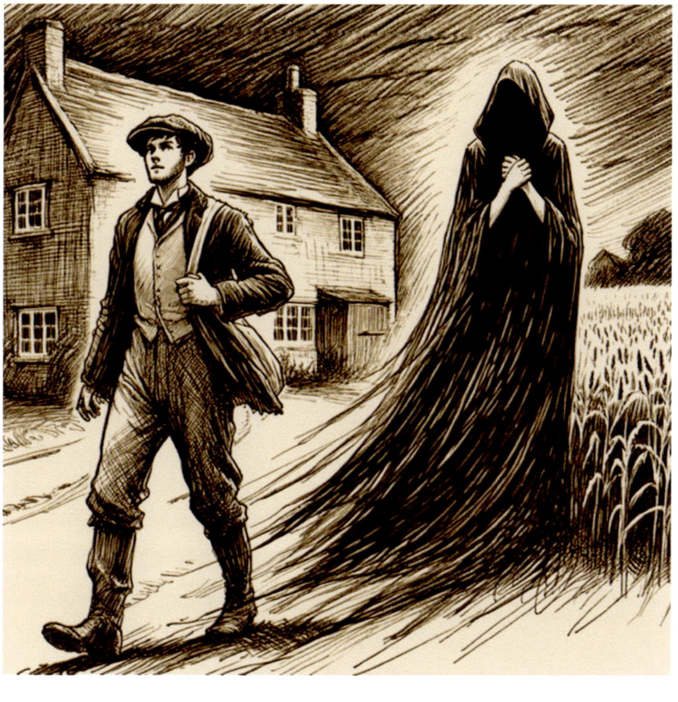

Although Sid never saw the ghost for himself, others say they saw her cloaked figure nearby.

Wolverhampton

Our final chapter takes place in Wolverhampton, the only city in the Black Country, where the metalworking and engineering industries that fuelled its expansion during the Industrial Revolution still form a significant part of the local economy. The city centre boasts a range of Victorian and Edwardian buildings, reflecting its prosperity during the nineteenth and early twentieth centuries, among which is the Grand Theatre, with its impressive Victorian facade. The theatre is rumoured to be haunted by at least two ghosts, including Mr Percy Purdy, a manager from the early twentieth century who still keeps a watchful eye on his theatre. Another spectral inhabitant is the ghost of a lady who allegedly died after falling from the stage or the boxes above. She is never seen or heard, but makes her presence known through the strong scent of the lavender perfume she was known to wear in life.

Another of the city's famous ghosts is Claude, who some believe had connections with the Grand Theatre. Claude haunts the railway station, opened in 1852, and is often seen by witnesses either waiting on platform four or riding the trains. He is

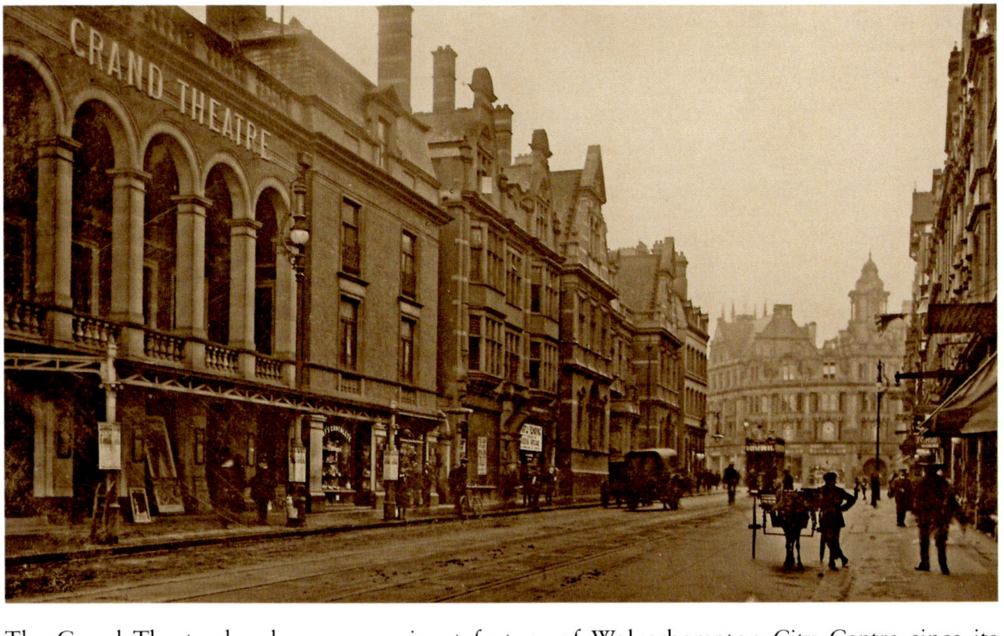

The Grand Theatre has been a prominent feature of Wolverhampton City Centre since its opening in 1894 and appeared on postcards such as this one posted in 1921.

described as a smartly dressed Victorian man wearing a top hat, appearing so vividly that unsuspecting witnesses often mistake him for an actor in costume.

However, our brief journey through the borough of Wolverhampton begins in the nearby town of Bilston, where one of its former residents was more feared in life than his ghost could ever be.

Bilston's Darkest Son

The ghostly tales woven into the fabric of the Black Country often draw less from the demonic and more from the coal-powered echoes of its industrial past. Hell Lane, The Fiery Holes Inn, and The Blazing Stump are names forged in the furnaces that once dominated this landscape, and amidst the orange glow of the Bilston skyline, the shadow of one man loomed ominously over the town.

By his early twenties, the dark deeds of Abel Hill had become infamous throughout the Bradley district. A labourer by day and a heavy drinker by night, Hill, a brash, arrogant womaniser, seduced Mary, the daughter of the house of his favourite haunt, the Old Bush Inn. Within a year, they were living together, but things turned sour between the couple when Mary gave birth to their son, Thomas. The weight of responsibility proved too heavy for Abel, who disowned Thomas, and an eventual maintenance order of two shillings only fuelled his resentment. When Mary fell pregnant again the following year, Abel attempted to snuff out the flame of new life by forcing Mary to drink what she described as a most vile-tasting medicine. Yet, when this plan failed, Abel concocted a more ghastly scheme.

Under the veil of night, he lured Mary and their young son to the quiet towpath by Glasshouse Bridge under the pretence of purchasing a hat and frock for the infant. There, under the cold gaze of the moon, he plunged them into the canal's murky waters, pinning them down with a boat hook until the struggle was over and the waters stilled once more. A fisherman's grim discovery the following morning brought Bilston's darkest son to swift justice. Arrested and confined, Abel could only watch

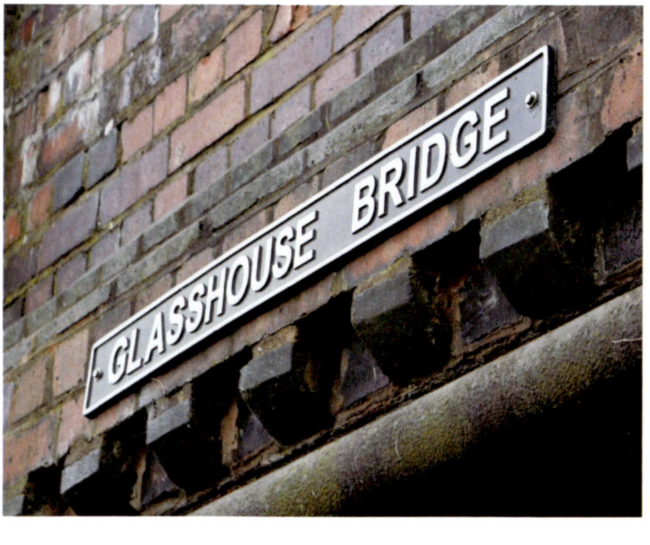

from a barred window as the cortege bearing the coffins of his wife and child trudged by. It is said he spat upon Mary's casket in a vile salute that sealed his infamy.

He was condemned to the gallows in Stafford, where, in July 1820, a huge crowd, peppered with many who had travelled from Bilston, came to see their infamous villain meet his demise. The deed was done, and with the noose still taut around his neck, the lifeless body of Abel Hill was returned to Bilston for dissection under the judge's order.

Legends murmured that his bones, secreted away in a sombre black box, came to rest in the attic of the Bilston Workhouse, where he toiled in life. Perhaps it was defiance, or a soul too corrupt even for hell, that bound Abel's spectre to the mortal realm. From a workhouse window, the pale face of his apparition, hollow-eyed and noose still present, was said to peer at troubled onlookers on the street below. Apparently not confined to the resting place of his bones, his ghost was also seen roaming the Old Firestone Pit pub, amidst the shadows where he and the miners once sought respite.

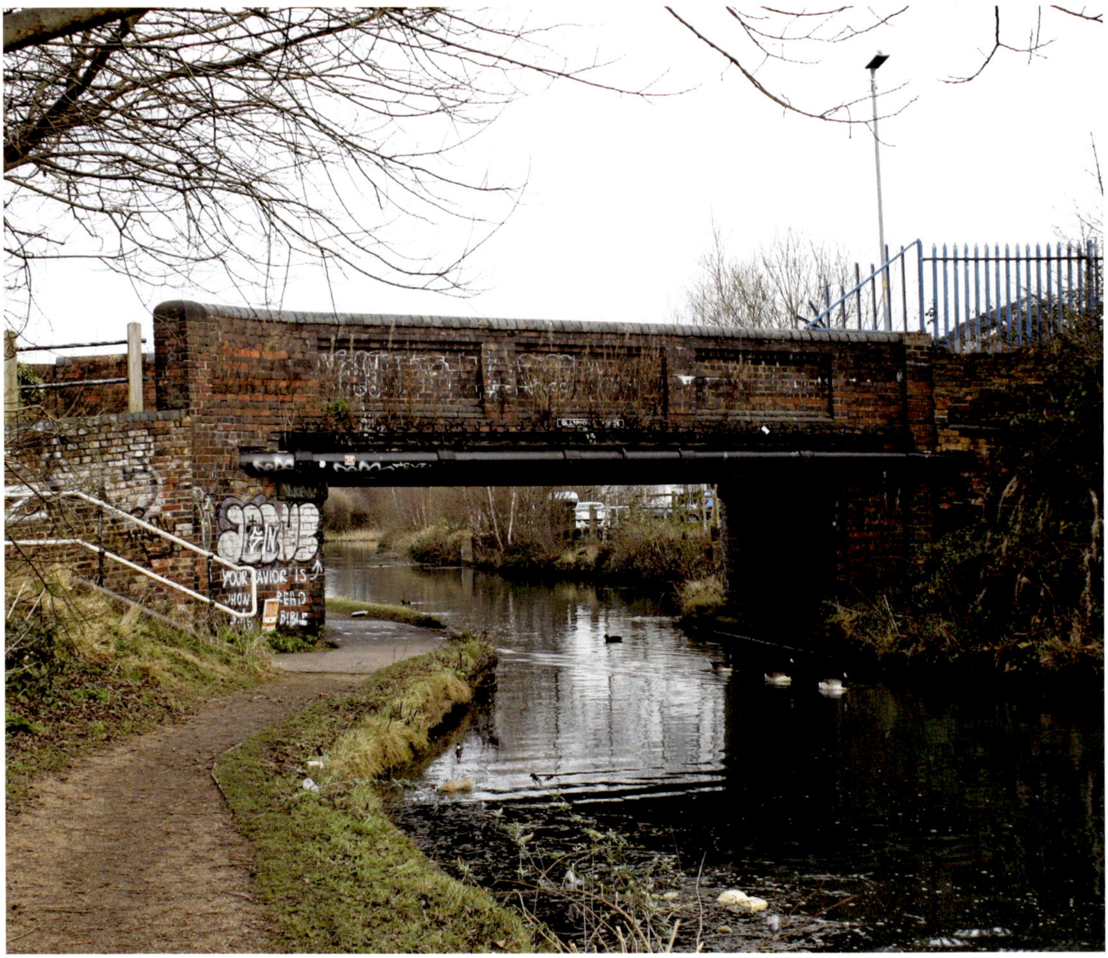

Glasshouse Bridge, the scene of Abel's terrible crime.

Beldray Ltd

After the boom of the Industrial Revolution, Beldray Ltd emerged as a hallmark of impeccable craftsmanship in the manufacture of a variety of metal homewares. From glistening copper kettles and galvanised buckets to decorative fruit bowls, each item bore its iconic bell logo, symbolising heritage and excellence. From its foundation in 1872 to its demise in 2005, the clink and clatter of manufacturing echoed around their Mount Pleasant works. Yet throughout its later history, amidst the din of hammers and hisses of steam, tales of a presence – not on the payroll – circulated among those who worked there. According to former worker George Philpott, a ghostly encounter in 1946 captured the attention of both the entire workforce and the local community.

One fateful night, a watchman's usual rounds took an uncanny turn. Silhouetted against the dim factory light, a figure draped in white seemed to hover near a flight of steps leading to the on-site bowling green. As the watchman cautiously approached for a closer look, the entity disappeared noiselessly upwards into the night sky. Shocked, the watchman left early that night and, for some time after, refused to go near the bowling green again. Word of the encounter spread like wildfire, and soon, night shifters began to notice a distant phantom figure vanishing into the sky whenever they drew near. The tale piqued such curiosity that both locals and *Express & Star* reporters gathered nightly at the factory gates on Willenhall Road, hoping for a glimpse of the otherworldly.

Determined to unravel the mystery of the Beldray Ghost, four intrepid members of the works staff embarked on a ghost hunt. Armed with a pistol and Dutch courage from a bottle of scotch, the men lay silently in wait, hiding by the bowling green haunt of this ghostly apparition. By morning, the mystery of the Beldray Ghost had been solved. The ghost turned out to be a large white barn owl gliding silently from its favourite perch – one of the pillars on the steps leading to the bowling green – thereby giving the appearance of a floating, legless figure.

The tale of the barn owl failed to quench the factory's thirst for the supernatural. Many workers spoke of hearing inexplicable bumps and sudden bangs, and of seeing shadowy figures around the building. The ladies' toilets by the works offices was an

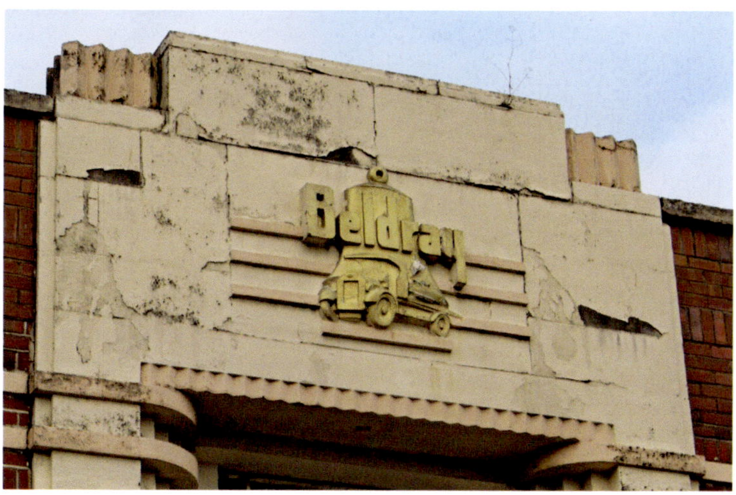

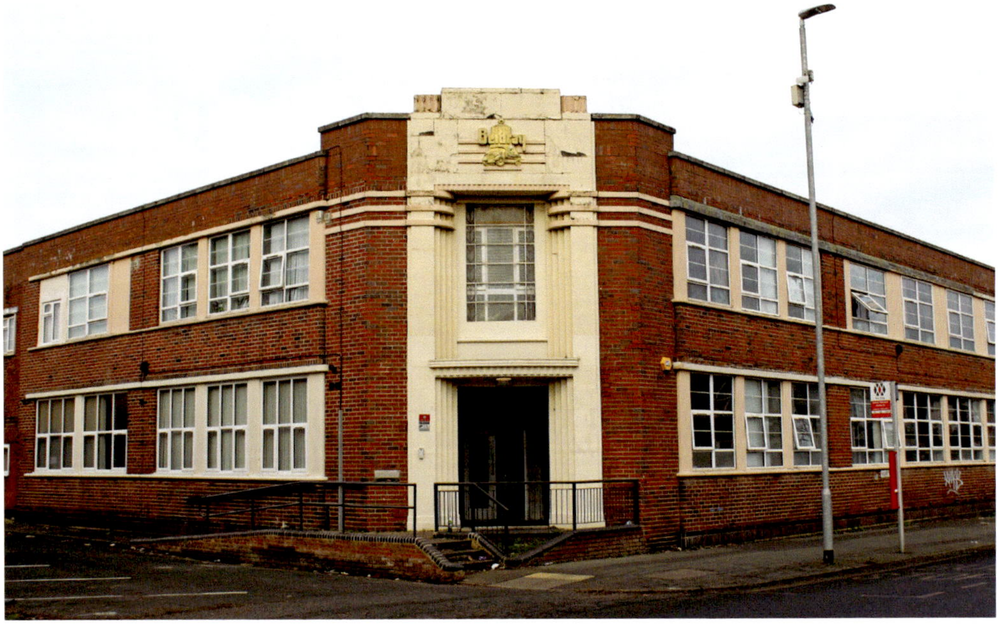

The Beldray building is now used by Wolverhampton Council but still bears the firm's iconic logo.

area many workers were convinced was haunted. Several of the female workers chose not to lock the cubicle doors, fearing a hasty retreat might be necessary. Mostly, the ghosts were heard by security workers, including one who said that after closing time, the building fell silent until around 10 or 11 p.m., when knocks and loud bangs with no discernible source could be heard. A radio stored in one of the rooms was also said to turn itself on in the middle of the night, and, despite being regularly checked, security alarms were sometimes activated for no apparent reason. Another security guard, Brian Davies, said that for him and many others who worked there, the ghosts were very real. Around 1977, Brian recalled, a security officer was convinced he saw the ghost of Hermon Bradley, a former chairman, emerge from an old garage, twenty-three years after his death. The security officer fled, leaving Brian to explain to the board of directors that they no longer had adequate overnight security because their nightwatchman had seen a ghost.

In 2005 silence fell over the factory, bringing an end to an era of manufacturing on the site.

The Giffard Arms

In mid-November, bad weather is expected, but on my journey to one of Wolverhampton's reputedly most haunted buildings, Storm Cairan brought a tempestuous atmosphere to its centre. Gale-force winds howled between the buildings on Victoria Street, and heavy raindrops danced off the pavement around my feet as I approached the Gothic facade of the Giffard Arms. Built in an early Tudor style, its

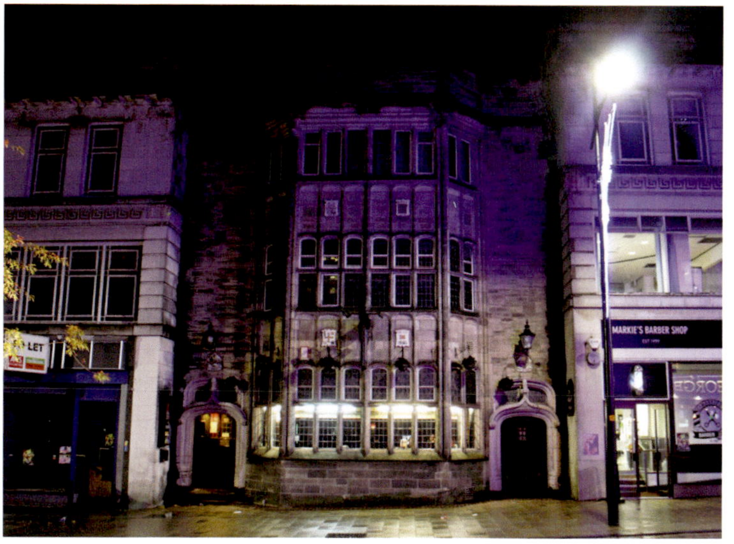

The imposing facade of the Giffard Arms on a stormy November night.

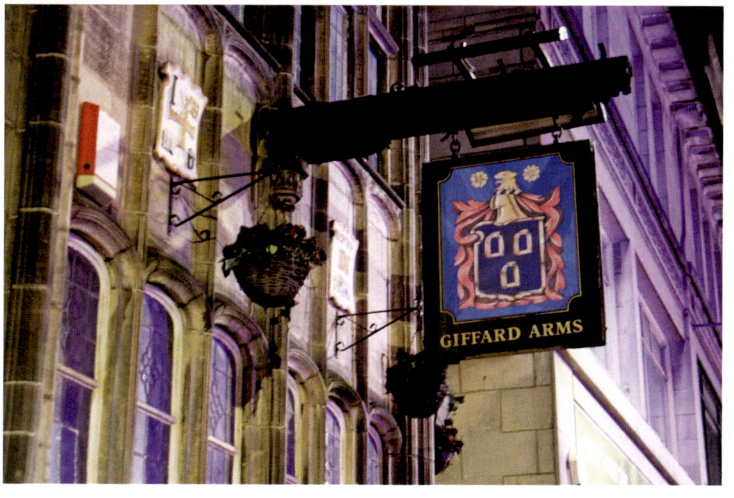

finely carved ashlar masonry and stained-glass windows, adorned with the Giffard family crest, contrast sharply with its contemporary surroundings. Thinking a bolt of lightning would be the only addition to make the scene more dramatic, I stepped through one of its large, arched doorways.

Inside, the atmosphere was equally captivating. Dark oak beams set against blood-red walls were adorned with Latin texts, skulls, and other eerie embellishments. Dim lighting and a large throne with dragon skull armrests completed the unique ambience. The staff, including the friendly and welcoming landlady, Wendy Shone, who has been there since 2003, warmed the atmosphere. Wendy took me to a quiet corner of the lounge, where we sat at a coffin-shaped table, complete with nails around its edge. She built the table with a friend not long after taking over the Giffard Arms, starting the transformation from a tired, nondescript pub to the charismatic and popular venue it is today.

This wasn't the building's first significant change. The facade, built in 1922, is much newer than its early Tudor appearance suggests. This style is a hallmark of architect J. A. Swan, who was commissioned for the current building, replacing an earlier inn. The original building, believed to be part of the Giffard family estate, served as a townhouse before becoming an inn. It's from this era that the pub's most famous ghost originates.

A few years ago, during a paranormal night, Wendy recounted, the hour was getting late and expecting the group of visiting paranormal enthusiasts to be wrapping up and heading home, she went to an upstairs room where they were set up. To her embarrassment, she accidentally set off all the motion-detecting alarms the group had positioned in the hallway. At that moment, the group was conducting one last séance for the night. Suddenly the temperature in the room dropped to an icy chill. Through the doorway emerged a figure, which failed to trigger the motion-detecting alarms. Wendy described the apparition as opaque, making it hard to discern details, but she was certain it was the figure of an adult lady, her hands gently resting on the shoulders of a child. The apparitions stood still, surveying the room, before vanishing. Wendy believes this may have been the ghost of Anne Haughton. Legend has it that Anne was a prostitute who frequented the earlier version of the Giffard Arms over a hundred years ago. Among her many clients was a member of the aristocratic Giffard family, the owners of the building. Anne reportedly gave birth to his child, leading

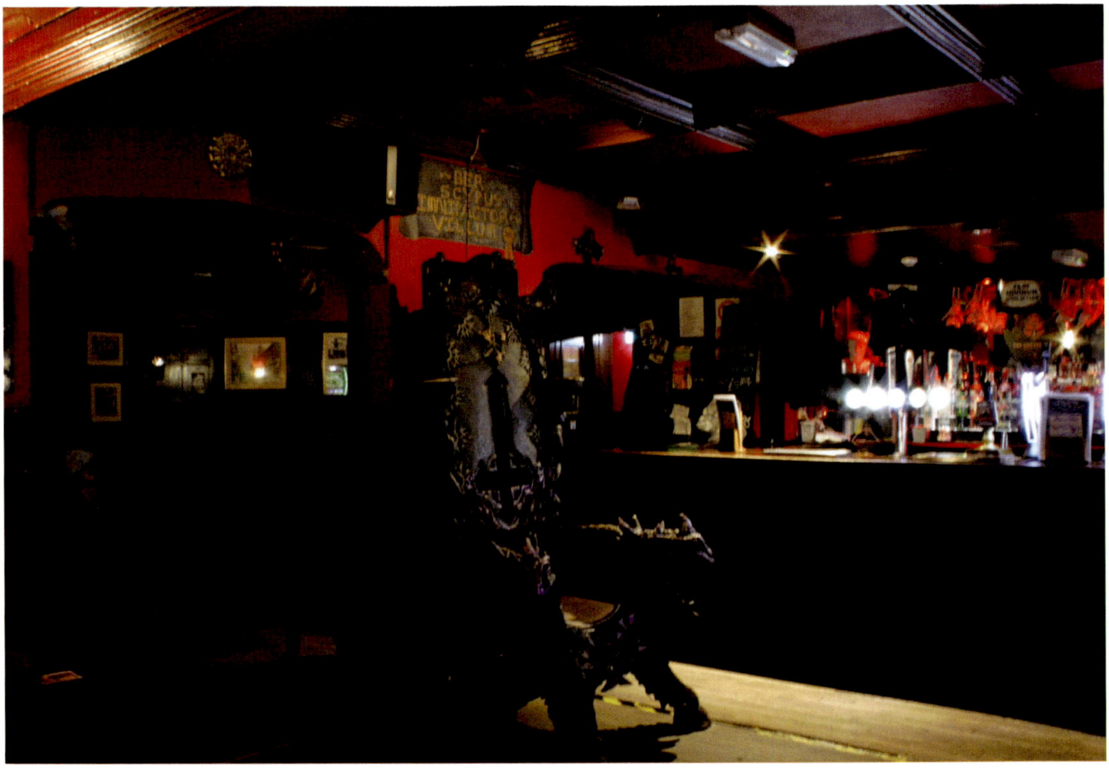

The pub is adorned with many features that add to its unique character, including the blood-red walls and large throne chair, creating an atmospheric space.

to their murder to hide the scandal and protect the family's reputation. However, Wendy suspects Anne was not a prostitute but rather his mistress. The truth remains shrouded in mystery, but sightings of a female apparition in the building are frequent and undeniable.

Another frequent ghost at the Giffard Arms is that of a young girl, first spotted by one of the venue's DJs, who lived in a room above the building. Puzzled, he came downstairs, asking Wendy, 'Who is the girl playing with bricks upstairs?'

Together, they searched but found no one. The ghost was next seen in the lounge on the ground floor, where a patron was startled by the sight of a young girl playing with bricks in a corner.

Other ghosts rumoured to haunt the Giffard include a small dog, seen running from one side of the lounge to the other before vanishing, and the ghost of a former landlord. Wendy admits she has not seen these herself, but others claim the landlord walks through the bar as if it wasn't there, possibly because the bar's location was different in his time.

One morning, more recently, the staff at the Giffard discovered books and paperwork scattered on the floor behind the bar. Reviewing the security camera footage, they expected to see a burglar. Astonishingly, the footage showed books and papers leaping off the shelf. Despite the initial shock of this event and other spooky sightings by staff and visitors, Wendy feels no fear of the ghosts. She considers them residents of the Giffard Arms, welcome to stay for as long as they wish.

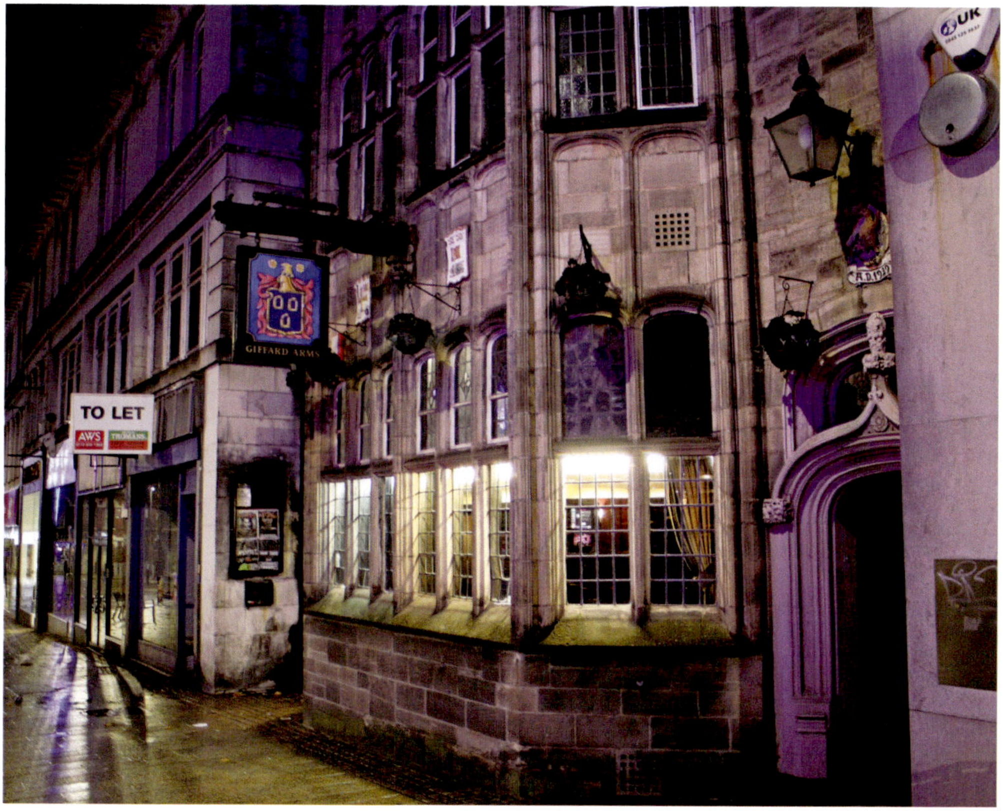

End

And there, our journey through the Black Country, and its tales of the paranormal, come to an end. Yet, across this influential region, many more stories are undoubtedly waiting to be told, so perhaps a second edition will need to happen. Until then, I will simply say, thank you, for joining me on my tour of the *Paranormal Black Country*.

Bibliography

Books

Homer, A., *Black Country Ghosts and Hauntings* (Tin Typewriter Publishing, 2017)
Poulton-Smith, A., *Black Country Ghosts* (The History Press Ltd, 2008)
Bills, D. M. & E. and W. R. Griffiths, *Kinver Rock Houses* (Elda Publications, 1978)
Solomon, P., *Haunted Black Country* (The History Press Ltd, 2009)
Bell, D., *Ghosts & Legends of Staffordshire & The Black Country* (Countryside Books, 1994)
Hawthorne, B., *Black Country & Birmingham Ghost Stories* (Bradwell Books, 2013)
Bradford, A., *The Haunted Midlands* (Brewin Books Ltd, 2006)
Symonds, R., *Diary of the Marches of the Royal Army During the Great Civil War* (Camden Society, 1859)

Newspapers

Birmingham Mail
Birmingham Gazette
Birmingham Evening Despatch
Birmingham Evening Mail
Black Country Evening Mail
Black Country Bugle
Sandwell Evening Mail
Walsall Observer
South Staffordshire Chronicle
Express & Star
The Guardian
Sunday Mercury (Birmingham)
Evening Mail (West Bromwich)
Evening Despatch (Birmingham)
The Birmingham Post
The Spokesman Review (Spokane, Washington)
The Ottawa Citizen (Ottawa, Canada)
The Daily Telegraph (London)

Websites

https://lisaandherworld-lisah.blogspot.com/
https://www.spookyisles.com/
https://localhistories.org/
https://lostwolverhampton.co.uk/
https://en.wikipedia.org/
https://historicengland.org.uk/
http://www.historywebsite.co.uk/
https://www.stourbridgenews.co.uk/
https://www.mysteriousbritain.co.uk/
https://weatherspark.com/
https://www.blackcountrysociety.com/